ACADEMIC ECONOMICS IN HOLLAND 1800–1870

STUDIES
IN SOCIAL LIFE
XIII

EDITOR:
GUNTHER BEYER

ACADEMIC
ECONOMICS IN HOLLAND
1800-1870

by

IRENE HASENBERG BUTTER

THE HAGUE
MARTINUS NIJHOFF
1969

PRINTED IN THE NETHERLANDS

TABLE OF CONTENTS

PREFACE

The present study is based on research largely pursued in Holland from December 1956 until July 1957. The inquiry is centered around the development of academic economics in Holland between 1800 and 1870. This period suggested itself as an appropriate unit of time though it became necessary to extend the specified period in certain parts of the study. Reasons for the temporal delimitation of the investigation will become apparent, as will the reasons for concentrating on academic economics.

Financial assistance from the Rockefeller Foundation helped to make possible the field research carried out in The Netherlands. Most of the material incorporated into the study was found in the following Dutch libraries: Bibliotheek der Nederlandsche Economische Hoogeschool, Rotterdam; Economische-Historische Bibliotheek, Amsterdam; Universiteitsbibliotheek van Amsterdam; Handels-Economische Bibliotheek, Amsterdam; and Koninklijke Bibliotheek, Den Haag. The study was greatly enhanced by suggestions and kind assistance from a number of librarians in charge of the above libraries.

I further wish to acknowledge cooperation of Professors J. H. Van Stuijvenberg, I. J. Brugmans, A. M. De Jong, P. Hennipman, G. M. Verrijn Stuart, and F. De Vries, who helped to direct my explorations when sources on Dutch economics were largely unfamiliar to me. Helpful advice and suggestions were supplied also by Drs. G. Koen, Drs. Joh. De Vries, and Drs. H. H. Behrens.

I am especially thankful to Professor H. W. Lambers of the Nederlandsche Economische Hoogeschool, whose advice, support, and encouragement were indispensable to the carrying out of this study. To a notable extent my stay in Holland was rewarding and beneficial because of Professor Lambers' continuous interest.

Professor Joseph J. Spengler, my supervisor, provided stimulation and encouragement at all stages of this inquiry. The study was conceived, conducted, and completed with Professor Spengler's guidance and support. To him I am uncommonly indebted for constructive criticism which resulted in improvements throughout the dissertation, and beyond that, for inspiration which he imparted throughout the years of my graduate study.

I. H. B.

CHAPTER I

INTRODUCTION

During the past two centuries the history of economic thought has received relatively little attention in Holland. The development of Dutch economics in particular rarely evoked curiosity among Dutch economists. Remarkably enough a German economist, Wilhelm Roscher, first stimulated interest in Dutch economic thought by suggesting that a prize be awarded for the best study on this topic. Etienne Laspeyres, a German scholar, conducted the earliest inquiry into Dutch economic ideas in response to Roscher's suggestion.[1] His book on the economic literature of the Netherlands was written in German and published in 1863. The appearance of Laspeyres' work motivated Otto Van Rees, one of Holland's well-known economists during the nineteenth century, to write a history of Dutch economic thought in the Dutch language, ready for publication in 1865.[2] Both studies were devoted to seventeenth and eighteenth century economic thought in the Netherlands; they constitute almost the whole of the literature having to do with Dutch economic ideas.

The purpose of the present study is to survey and analyze the development of Dutch economics during the nineteenth century. The writer, in undertaking this inquiry, did not expect to uncover hidden treasures or to reinstate neglected contributions. There was no reason to expect challenges or discoveries of this nature, even though the territory covered was largely unfamiliar. The dominant theme which underlies the presentation of material in

[1] Etienne Laspeyres, *Geschichte der Volkswirtschaftlichen Anschauungen der Niederlaender* (Leipzig, 1863).
[2] Otto Van Rees, *Geschiedenis der Staathuishoudkunde in Nederland* (Utrecht, 1865).

this study is the growth of economics as an autonomous branch of knowledge – the emancipation of economics from the law faculties of universities as well as the professionalization of economists engaged outside of universities.

The period covered ranges roughly from 1800 to 1870. This time span was selected for the following reasons: the development of Dutch economic thought between 1800 and 1870 can be broken down into two phases: (1) introduction and adoptation of mostly liberal economic ideas from England, France, and Germany; and (2) ideas, developed or imported, in response to practical problems faced by the Dutch economy. After 1870 changes of both sorts took place. The mid 1870's marked the inception of Austrian economics in Holland, and for a while Dutch economists were more strongly oriented toward the Austrian school than to any other foreign school of thought. This in itself changed the nature of economic investigation in Holland, shifting emphasis to value theory and abstract-theoretical analyses. Furthermore, around 1870 the Dutch economy underwent some very basic changes, which altered the character of the economic problems that largely shaped the content of Dutch economic writings. By 1870 industrialization of the country had been well launched, a modern banking system was in operation, laborers had begun to organize into unions, monetary and fiscal problems had assumed a different character, and after 1880 even the role of the state had begun to re-expand.[3] Particularly during the last quarter of the century such problem areas as urbanization, population growth, wage and interest theory, economic fluctuations, and international trade, drew considerable attention; this had not been the case prior to 1870.

The period 1800 to 1870 represents a suitable unit of time for this study, especially with regard to the scope and level of economic inquiry and to the problems posed by the Dutch economy. With regard to the achievement of full autonomy for economics as a discipline, our study must extend into the twentieth century.

---

[3] I. J. Brugmans, "Honderd Jaren Nederlandsche Nijverheid, 1830–1930," in *Welvaart en Historie* ('s Gravenhage, 1950), p. 121; Hans Max Hirschfeld, *Het Ontstaan Van Het Moderne Bankwezen in Nederland* (Rotterdam, 1932); I. J. Brugmans, *De Arbeidende Klasse in Nederland in de 19e Eeuw* ('s Gravenhage, 1925), p. 268; Z. W. Sneller, *Geschiedenis van de Nederlandsche Landbouw 1795–1940* (Tweede Druk, Groningen, 1951), p. 37.

Though a certain degree of autonomy was achieved for the economic discipline within the period 1800 to 1870, the official emancipation of economics from control by university law faculties was not initiated until 1913, when the Rotterdam School of Economics was founded. This event was not unrelated to nineteenth century developments in economic thought and practice. Since the main theme of the present study revolves around the evolution of economics into an independent branch of knowledge, the chapter concerned with the status of economics in the university structure could not, therefore, be confined within the shorter time span defined above. In general the period covered by this inquiry can only be delineated approximately inasmuch as the activities of some leading economists of the period extended beyond the year 1870.[4]

The writer has concentrated on what was thought to be a representative group of academic economists. Emphasis on academic economists suggested itself because the development of academic economics had been selected as the central topic of the study. Yet, because all nineteenth century Dutch economists were trained to be lawyers, a definition of academic economist was called for. He is, for the purposes of this study, a person who, for a considerable part of his life, was involved in one or more activities directly related to the use or to the development of economics as a body of scientific and/or applied knowledge. Those economists who spent the major part of their lives teaching and contributing to the professional literature comprise the representative group of economists. Writers who were not engaged in academic roles, or to whom economics was secondary to another field such as law, political science, or sociology, have not been considered unless they contributed to the discussion of a leading topic. It is believed that this selectivity does not result in significant omissions, or in a distorted view of Dutch economics in general.

A considerable part of the study will focus on the cultural, political, and economic context in which nineteenth century Dutch economics developed rather than on economic thought per se. It was felt that the contextual factors relevant to economic

---

[4] N. G. Pierson has not been included in this study as a major figure since Pierson's contributions were made principally after 1870. His participation in the currency-banking controversy could not be ignored, however, and his views on earlier Dutch economists have also been incorporated.

thinking were nearly as important as the economic ideas themselves, particularly for an understanding of progress or stagnation in this field of knowledge. In Chapters II and III a sketch of the historical background of the period has been attempted as well as a description of the structure and development of the Dutch economy during the period covered. Chapter III has to do also with some non-academic economic views, particularly those of a King and of a cabinet member in Holland in the early part of the nineteenth century. In Chapter IV the structure of higher education is examined with respect to the role and status of economics in Dutch universities. Certain deterrents to the development of economics were found to be inherent in the rules and in the structure of higher educational institutions. Chapter V has been devoted to more personal factors; it is based largely on biographical information respecting the professional lives of representative Dutch economists. It thus was possible to examine the status of economics as a professional field and to observe certain changes relevant to its professionalization.

Chapters VI and VII, respectively, are devoted to the nature of Dutch economic thought and to foreign impacts on Dutch economists. In Chapter VI the major writings of our representative group are examined with respect to the relative importance of economic history, economic theory, and applied economics in nineteenth-century Dutch economic inquiry. Chapter VII reveals Dutch eclecticism respecting economic ideas of foreign origin. A list of Dutch translations of foreign books on economics is presented in an appendix to Chapter VII.

Certain topics which were excluded from the study may also be mentioned here. Ideas of Dutch economists regarding the colonies have not been considered, since colonial thought would comprise a study in itself. Socialist tendencies in Dutch economic thought largely post-dated the period under consideration and have therefore been omitted; the representative economists here considered were generally hostile to socialism.

CHAPTER II

THE DUTCH ECONOMY: 1600–1870

The period during which the Dutch economy reached its heyday included roughly the seventeenth and early eighteenth centuries. By the late eighteenth century the most flourishing and most adventurous course of economic development for Holland was a thing of the past, which had left a vivid and profound imprint on people's minds and attitudes. The fact that the Dutch "Golden Age" took place during the seventeenth and eighteenth centuries together with the nature of this striking phase in Dutch economic history is relevant to Dutch economic development in the nineteenth century and to our understanding of certain aspects of economic thought in that period. A sketch of the economic history of the Netherlands prior to the nineteenth century as well as of the period 1800 to 1870 will be presented in this chapter.

The Dutch economy is conditioned by its geographical situation to an extraordinary extent. This was particularly obvious during its period of economic supremacy, when the Netherlands, located roughly between northern and southern regions of Europe and without notable transportation barriers to the East, developed an enormous staple and carrying trade. Being relatively poor in both agricultural and other resources Holland had to develop, in response to its own needs, a large fishing fleet and a vast trading fleet.

Holland's capacity for industrial development was limited by its shortage of most resources. The industries which developed during its early history usually owed their existence to a close connection with trade. Only small areas of the soil were suitable for the growing of grains. On the other hand, cattle raising and the cultivation of dairy products were practiced with considerable success.[1] Proximity to long stretches of sea coupled with rivers for inland transportation, as well as an early dependence on all sorts of imports, launched the country on a course eventuating in the dominance of shipping and trading in the Dutch economy.

Holland's outstanding trading aptitude was thus at least partly determined by its geography. But the supremacy of its trading position, as well as the high level of prosperity [2] achieved during the seventeenth and eighteenth centuries, were in part attributable to opportunities of transient nature. European trade at that time did not lend itself readily to direct, bilateral exchanges; it was organized into a multilateral system of commerce, with Holland, easily accessible to most parts of Europe, serving as the intermediate center of distribution. The special attributes of Holland, together with the need for a central market within Holland, thus were responsible for the supremacy of the status which Amsterdam quite suddenly acquired in the seventeenth century in world trade. For, as shipping center, commodity market, and capital market, Amsterdam became the metropolis of European commerce, with other Dutch cities carrying on related activities on a minor scale.

During the seventeenth and part of the eighteenth centuries then, Holland was the magnetic center of the world network of commerce, and its magnetic field extended from Norway to Italy and Portugal, as well as from England to Russia. Furthermore, its

---

[1] Ernst Baasch, *Hollaendische Wirtschaftsgeschichte* (Jena, 1927), pp. 1–2.

[2] Figures indicative of relative levels of prosperity of England, France, and Holland in 1688 and in 1695 were presented by Gregory King, and represent the only figures the writer is aware of:

1688

	Population	Nat. Income	Net Saving
England	5,500,000	43,500,000 £	1,800,000 £
France	14,000,000	84,000,000	5,000,000
Holland	2,200,000	17,750,000	2,000,000

1695

	Population	Nat. Income	Net Saving
England	5,450.000	42,500,000 £	3,000,000 £ Decr.
France	13,500,000	74,000,000	6,000,000 Decr.
Holland	2,240,000	18,250,000	850,000 Incr.

In 1695 while England and France were dissaving, the Dutch still managed to save. See Gregory King, *Naturel and Political Observations and Conclusions upon the State and Condition of England.* 1696 (reprinted by the Johns Hopkins Press, Baltimore, 1936), p. 55.

magnetic field included trade with the colonies. Holland's carrying trade distributed products from the Dutch colonies all over Europe, and handled a sizable proportion of the goods coming from British colonies as well.[3]

The list of goods around which the Dutch carrying trade was organized is almost innumerable. Among the major items were grain, timber, metals and ammunition from the North, and fine laces, textiles and linens from Belgium and France; while from Spain and Italy came wines, wool, silks and the like. In addition there was the colonial trade which revolved around spices, cotton, tea, indigo, sugar, and tobacco. Nonetheless, the Dutch were not merely monopolists of the carrying trade in consequence of their incomparably low freight charges. The centrality of their position in the world of commerce, as will be noted, rested also upon other bases.

Intermediary trading functions were well developed in Holland, since many goods entered the country only to be re-exported. The merchants who carried on this intermediary trade comprised a group of specialists skilled in the performance of marketing and stapling functions. They were experts in the appraisal of merchandise, for they possessed extensive information and had a good perspective of market conditions all over the world. There was also a sizable group of so-called "Second Hand" merchants, who bought goods in order to inspect, sort, package or store them, either for eventual re-sale to Dutch wholesalers for domestic consumption or to wholesalers from other countries. The activities of these "Second Hand" merchants, which grew out of Holland's role as an international commodity center, were indispensable to a multilateral system of trade in non-standardized products. Speculative commodity transactions were executed on the Bourse, founded in 1611, The Amsterdam Bank, founded in 1609, represented a reliable center for the clearance of payments. Weekly price lists had been circulated at least since 1585, and served as standard indices for all of commercial Europe.[4] A generous supply of credit, made available, as a rule, by Dutch

[3] Charles Wilson, *Anglo-Dutch Commerce & Finance In the Eighteenth Century* (Cambridge, 1941), p. 10.

[4] Violet Barbour, *Capitalism in Amsterdam in the Seventeenth Century*, The Johns Hopkins University Studies in Historical and Political Science, Series LXVII, 1950 (Baltimore, 1950), p. 20.

merchants, was an additional attraction to foreign businessmen. In short, all functions accessorial to trade, such as brokerage, the supply of storage and packing services, insurance, exchange, and credit facilities, were developed in Holland to a higher degree than anywhere else, during the seventeenth century.

At the same time that the Dutch economy was excelling commercially it was also maintaining a high level of industrial activity. Economic historians conventionnally divide the Dutch industries of that time into two categories: (1) independent or autonomous industries, like the textile industry, which pre-dated the development of the Dutch economy into a center of world commerce; and (2) the industries which had originated entirely as a result of Dutch commercial activities ("trafieken"), such as the finishing and refining industries. Thus the grain trade gave rise to malting, brewing, and distilling. Tobacco cutting, tanning, and sugar refining, as well as cotton printing, dyeing, and bleaching exemplify industries dependent upon and arising out of the staple market. Dutch shipping had given rise also to a number of important derivative industries such as ship building, rope making and the manufacturing of sails.[5] It is evident from the above that the commercial and the industrial activities of the Dutch seventeenth century economy were interdependent to a very large extent.

As previously mentioned, Holland's economic supremacy during the seventeenth and part of the eighteenth century was at least partly attributable to opportunities of a temporary nature. These opportunities existed only so long as conditions of economic backwardness predominated in neighboring countries. But after the year 1730 it became increasingly apparent that the Dutch monopoly in transport and commerce had been seriously weakened by the economic development taking place in other countries and by the accompanying growth of direct trade relationships. The magnetic center in the end lost most of its power, with the result that Holland's intermediary function of channeling trade and of centering the final impact of the international supply of and demand for goods within the Netherlands was greatly reduced in importance.

---

[5] Tjalling Pieter Van Der Kooy, *Hollands Stapelmarkt En Haar Verval* (Amsterdam 1931), pp. 8–10. For a detailed account see Baasch, *op. cit.*, pp. 101–155.

Among the factors which helped to bring about a gradual but persisting decline in the Dutch economy in the eighteenth century the following stand out:

(1) The development of mercantilistic policy within Western European nations, directed at the achievement of maximum economic self-sufficiency and domestic industrial expansion.[6] This policy undermined Dutch economic supremacy in two ways: (a) through the restrictions imposed on Dutch imports; (b) through the establishment of direct trading routes and the consequent building up of competition in shipping services and port facilities. The old intermediary trade became restricted to war time, when other nations were unable to engage in direct commercial transactions.

(2) Failure to counterbalance decline in the Dutch central stapling market by the development of domestic industries. The shift of commercial activity away from Holland brought along with it a contraction in finishing and refining industries dependent on the staple market for the supply of raw materials and market outlets.

(3) In the late eighteenth century Holland's colonial monopoly was gradually undermined, especially by the growth of British trade with the colonies, but also by competition from such countries as France, Spain, Portugal, Sweden, and Denmark.[7]

(4) Gradually financial activities began to supersede commercial activities and the Dutch merchants became bankers. Though the Dutch still financed an important part of the world trade, goods were no longer stapled and transported by the merchants of Holland. Savings of the Dutch people were channeled at least partly into foreign loans rather than into the development of Dutch industries.[8]

---

[6] Though England and France had made attacks on Holland's commercial supremacy during the seventeenth century (English Navigation Acts, Colbert's tariffs of 1664 and 1667), these proved to be premature; they failed to penetrate Holland's monopoly of intermediary trade until at least 1730. Charles Wilson, "The Economic Decline of the Netherlands," *The Economic History Review*, IX, No. 2 (May 1939), 111.

[7] Van der Kooy, *op. cit.*, p. 43.

[8] Wilson, "The Economic Decline of the Netherlands," *op. cit.*, p. 113. The figures of Gregory King, presented on p. 11, indicate a high savings potential for Holland during the seventeenth century. In 1782 an estimate of Dutch savings was made by Van de Spiegel, who judged total Dutch savings to be 1 billion fl. See Huisarchief der Koningin, archief Willem V, no. 337, bundel 38, d.d. 7 Juni, 1782, cited by P. J. Blok, *Geschiedenis Van Het Nederlandsche Volk*, vol. 3, third edition, p. 569. For

Although warning signals of the decline in prospect appeared early in the eighteenth century, drastic signs of decay were not immediately evident in Holland's market behavior. The scene was one of a rapidly expanding volume of world trade, with Holland maintaining her own volume at a relatively constant level. At first, therefore, the Dutch trading position became weak only in relation to that of other nations whose trade was expanding. Clear evidence of the contraction of Dutch trade was available as early as 1751,[9] however, even though economic collapse did not take place until in the 1780's, when the accelerating economic development of Britain, together with the various wars Holland engaged in near the end of the century brought the golden era of the Dutch economy to a close. With the subsequent emergence of a new economic order, based upon iron and steel, the Dutch economy faced the task of seeking new sources of economic power.

At the beginning of the nineteenth century there were indications of a faint revival in certain areas of commerce, especially in the grain trade. This very limited upturn deluded the Dutch merchants into great expectations, of no less than a return of Holland's once glorious trading supremacy. Failure of these hopes to be realized was always attributed to causes other than the obsolescence of the once very important intermediary market function performed by Holland. In reality, wartime conditions had accelerated the emancipation of foreign traders from the Dutch stapling market, with the result that when peace was restored the skill and information which had been acquired independently in other countries, wiped out Holland's commercial superiority and the strategic character of her intermediary role.

Contraction of the Dutch economy during the late eighteenth

additional information on Dutch foreign investment see Charles Wilson, *Anglo-Dutch Commerce & Finance in the Eighteenth Century*; Alice Carter, "The Dutch and the English Public Debt in 1777," *Economica*, XX (1953), 159-162, and "Dutch Foreign Investment, 1738-1800," *ibid.*, pp. 322-341.

9 The "Propositie" of 1751: "Proposals Made By His late Highness the Prince of Orange to their High Mightiness the States-General And To The States Of Holland and West Friezland, For redressing and amending the Trade of the Republick," is included in J. R. McCulloch, *A Select Collection of Scarce and Valuable Tracts on Commerce* (London, 1859), pp. 426-480. This tract is a dissertation compiled by a group of "most intelligent and eminent merchants," in which they reviewed the causes of the decline of trade and possible means to restore trade. The merchants recommended the establishment of a limited free port and diminution of duties.

and early nineteenth centuries was not brought about solely by the outmoding of her commercial functions. The extinction of many of her industries added considerably to the difficulties of the general economic situation. When Holland sided with France in the war of 1795 against England, the country was pretty nearly cut off from the sea and consequently barred from acquiring raw material supplies.[10] Temporary loss of the Dutch colonies put additional restrictions upon the Dutch economy. As mentioned above, the domestic supply of raw materials was limited relative to the needs of domestic industries. For this reason the development and survival of many Dutch industries was largely dependent on Holland's advantages in obtaining foreign raw materials and on her contacts with foreign market outlets. The Napoleonic wars, therefore, had a detrimental effect on many of the country's most important industries. Of Holland's major industries the bleaching, calico-printing, silk, cotton and wool industries as well as the shipping, tanning, and Delft earthenware industries suffered extensively from raw material shortages and the blockade to export markets.[11]

Only a slight revival of these industries was possible after the wars had ended because the countries which formerly had imported from Holland had since undergone industrial development and consequently had ceased to be purchasers of Dutch merchandise. In addition, British export goods competed fiercely with the products of Dutch industries. The only Dutch exports which remained promising despite British competition were essentially agricultural, namely, butter, cheese, and madder. Indeed, continuing prosperity for Holland was largely restricted in the early nineteenth century to agriculture.

In 1813 when Holland regained her independence and her

[10] According to Pringsheim, export restrictions on raw materials practiced by European countries had an adverse effect on Dutch industries already late in the eighteenth century. There were restrictions on the export of raw wool in England, Brandenburg, Denmark, and Spain, and the export of raw silk was restricted in France and Italy (in the late seventeenth and early eighteenth centuries). Pringsheim reported that the Dutch manufacturing industries were dependent on Spanish wool, Indian, Chinese, and Italian Silk, and Norwegian timber. The Dutch East India Company moreover failed to supply a sufficient quantity of silk from the colonies during the middle of the eighteenth century. Otto Pringsheim, *Beitraege zur Wirtschaftlichen Entwicklungsgeschichte der Vereinigten Niederlande im 17. und 18. Jahrhundert* (Leipzig, 1890), pp. 38–40. Also see Van der Kooy, *op. cit.*, pp. 53–54.

[11] H. R. C. Wright, *Free Trade And Protection In The Netherlands 1816–1830* (Cambridge, 1955), pp. 35–42.

colonies, a period of state-supported economic reconstruction and reorientation began. It was the first time in Dutch history that use was made of an active economic policy which served as a unifying influence and which overrode the particularistic and multicity type of government which had characterized the Dutch Republic. The time span, 1813 to 1850, though a period of moderate mercantilism, actually prepared the country for eventual adoption of a consistent free trade policy. During the same period the Dutch-Belgian union was effected only to be dissolved subsequently. The ensuing period, 1850 to 1870, was one of preparation for Holland's industrial revolution which apparently had gotten well under way by 1870.

The active role of the state in reviving the Dutch economy in the early nineteenth century will be discussed in the next chapter. In this chapter the development in various sectors of the Dutch economy between 1800 and 1870 will be further examined. When Dutch commerce had become seriously depressed by the end of the eighteenth century, agriculture temporarily became the backbone of the Dutch economy. For the nourishment of its population as well as for the supply of export products the country depended almost entirely on its agricultural sector. Dairy products such as butter and cheese as well as potato meal and sugar constituted Holland's major exports early in the century. For this reason the Dutch were seriously concerned about British import duties on butter and cheese introduced in 1816. At that time three-fourths of the butter produced in the Northern Provinces was exported to England, whose demand for Holland's dairy products increased in the course of the century.[12]

Thus the Dutch economy specialized in dairy exports but was not self-sufficient in respect to the supply of grains needed to feed the population. Scarcity developed during the Napoleonic wars when Holland was partly cut off from its sources of supply. This gave rise to higher grain prices which continued until 1818. After 1818 grain prices tended downward until 1825. Holland's response to low grain prices by means of corn law legistaion will be

---

[12] Z. W. Sneller, *De Ontwikkeling Der Nederlandsche Export-Industrie* (Haarlem, 1925), p. 26; Z. W. Sneller, *Geschiedenis Van de Nederlandsche Landbouw 1795–1940*, pp. 38–39; N. W. Posthumus, *Documenten Betreffende De Buitenlandsche Handelspolitiek Van Nederland In De Negentiende Eeuw*, I ('s-Gravenhage, 1919), XIII–XIV; Baasch, *op. cit.*, pp. 490–491.

discussed in Chapter VI. After 1825 and until 1850 grain prices in Holland rose continuously though this was not the case in other European countries. Agricultural endeavors, therefore, became more profitable than most forms of economic activity undertaken in Holland between 1800 and 1850. According to Sneller, Brugmans and other economic historians, the Dutch economy, during the first half of the nineteenth century, did not advance beyond the agrarian stage.[13] However, agricultural exports, particularly dairy products and vegetables, continued to be of great significance to the Dutch economy, even after industrialization had gotten under way.

Inevitably the industrial sector of the economy was affected by the incidence of adverse circumstances upon Dutch commerce. The gradual decline of commerce, reenforced as it was by the Napoleonic wars, had greatly contracted most of Holland's important industries, but their recovery in the early nineteenth century proceeded very slowly. Among the factors responsible for the continuingly stagnant conditions of Dutch industry during the first half of the nineteenth century the following are remarkable:

(1) Holland's previously international trade had dwindled to "local trade."[14]

(2) Besides flax, coarse wool, peat and madder, Holland produced no industrial raw materials. Raw-material imports were burdened by the mercantilistic export duties imposed by raw material producing countries.[15]

(3) Holland lacked a heavy industry of the sort that usually tends to stimulate improvements in a country's industrial organization and technological development.[16]

(4) A pre-capitalistic mentality on the part of Dutch entrepreneurs manifested itself in the form of traditionalism, conservatism, lack of interest in innovation, or in the application of new inventions when these were available, and efforts to re-

[13] Baasch, op. cit., p. 487; I. J. Brugmans, "De Economische Conjunctuur in Nederland In De 19e Eeuw," in Welvaart en Historie, pp. 105–115; Z. W. Sneller, De Ontwikkeling Der Nederlandsche Export-Industrie, p. 19; I. J. Brugmans, "Honderd Jaren Nederlandsche Nijverheid, 1830–1930," op. cit., p. 118; Z. W. Sneller, Geschiedenis Van De Nederlandsche Landbouw 1795–1940, pp. 62–63.

[14] W. M. F. Mansvelt, Geschiedenis Van De Nederlandsche Handel-Maatschappij, I (Haarlem, 1924–1926), 35.

[15] Van der Kooy, op. cit., p. 53.

[16] Baasch, op. cit., p. 451.

install such outmoded institutions of the past as guilds; it was partly responsible for the persistence of small-scale, pre-factory industrial modes.[17]

(5) Dutch industries which managed to survive in the early nineteenth century were unable to compete in export markets because of excessively high labor costs. If commerce was to be free, revenues had to be raised from sources such as necessities, luxuries, and property. High taxes on necessities (for which Holland was notable), combined with a rising trend in food prices, resulted in high nominal wages, which handicapped Dutch industry. Real input costs were higher in Holland then in other countries furthermore, insofar as industry was technologically more efficient in these countries than in Holland.[18]

(6) During the early part of the nineteenth century a considerable part of Dutch industry moved into rural areas where the cost of living and, therefore, monetary wage costs were lower. This meant that Dutch industries were distributed throughout the country even though, given the poor communication channels of the time, so wide a dispersal of industry was not likely to promote industrial development. It was not until the 1860's that Dutch industry began to move back to cities and became geographically concentrated.[19]

(7) Holland also lagged behind other countries with regard to the development of means of transportation. Whereas England proceeded to introduce the use of steam into ocean transportation, the Dutch for some time refused to adapt themselves to the use of steam. Furthermore, the development of railroads in Holland did not become significant until in the second half of the nineteenth century.[20] All of the factors listed, along with others not mentioned here, served greatly to limit the development of Dutch industry throughout the first half of the century.

---

[17] I. J. Brugmans, *De Arbeidende Klasse In Nederland In De 19e Eeuw*, pp. 59–64.

[18] Brugmans reported that certain food prices rose at least 50 per cent between 1820 and 1870. *Ibid.*, pp. 136–137. Brugmans also claimed that while grain prices rose in Holland between 1825 and 1850, they tended downward in other countries; this disparity was partly responsible for the lethargy of Dutch industry during the period. I. J. Brugmans, "De Economische Conjunctuur In Nederland In De 19e Eeuw," *op. cit.*, p. 115. See also Van Der Kooy, *op. cit.*, p. 54, and Baasch, *op. cit.*, p. 451.

[19] Baasch, *op. cit.*, p. 452.

[20] Van Der Kooy, *op. cit.*, pp. 76–78. I. J. Brugmans, *De Arbeidende Klasse In Nederland In De 19e Eeuw*, pp. 69–72.

Only in the Belgian part of the Netherlands was industry progressing prior to 1830. When the Dutch-Belgian Union was dissolved in 1830, however, some salutary industrial changes began gradually to be made in Northern Holland. The Dutch textile industry is a case in point. After the Belgians were no longer allowed to export their textiles to the Dutch colonies, Willem I encouraged Belgian textile manufacturers to move their factories to Holland. They were thus enabled to maintain contact with market outlets situated in the Indies and at the same time to help Holland to establish a much needed export industry.[21] Other activities of King Willem I and the Netherland Trading Company, together with the growth of the textile industry, will be discussed in the next chapter. It may be noted here, however, that prior to the development of a metal industry after 1870 and of chemical and electrical industries in the twentieth century, textiles continued to be Holland's major industry.

Despite the remarkable industrial development that took place in the Dutch economy during the latter part of the nineteenth century, industrial production did not replace or overshadow other spheres of economic activity. Agriculture and trade, as well as industry, continued to be important sources of economic livelihood in Holland, though statistics on their relative contributions to the national income during the nineteenth century are mostly unavailable.[22] Holland's foreign trade revived during the second half of the century, especially after the commercial policy of various countries became increasingly liberal. Average annual

[21] I. J. Brugmans, "Honderd Jahren Nederlandsche Nijverheid, 1830–1930," *op. cit.*, p. 120.

[22] Kuznets has reported the following figures for the late eighteenth and early nineteenth centuries:
National Product, Current Prices, Percentage Distribution by Industry, Long-Term Series.
D. Netherlands – National Product

	Agricul. forestry & fish (1)	Industry (2)	All other (100.0-col. 1 & col. 2) (3)	Transp. (4)	Trade (5)	Public Adminis. (6)	Other serv- ices (7)
1789	49	18	33	12	5	9	7
1815	51	22	27	7	4	11	

Simon Kuznets, "Quantitative Aspects Of The Economic Growth of Nations," *Economic Development And Cultural Change*, V, No. 4 July, 1957, Appendix Table 2, p. 69. These were the only figures the writer was able to find regarding the nineteenth century.

imports increased from a value of: 311 Mil. fl. during 1857 to 1861 to 1887 Mil. fl. during 1897 to 1901, while average annual exports increased from a value of 246 Mil. fl. during 1857 to 1861 to 1601 Mil. fl. during 1897 to 1901. Holland's transit trade also expanded significantly after the 1870's, partly as a result of the development of the German hinterland.[23] Although Dutch commerce never resumed the predominant role it played in the seventeenth and early eighteenth centuries, it again developed into a significant sector of the economy.

Information concerning population and employment in Holland may serve to complement the picture given above of Holland's nineteenth-century economy. Holland's population as of 1803–1804 has been estimated at about 2,024,000. By 1829 its population is reported as approximating 2,427,000, but doubts are expressed respecting the accuracy of this figure.[24] Between 1815 and 1850 the Dutch population increased by about 38 per cent.[25] Decennial growth in Holland in representative decades has been reported as follows:[26]

> Between 1829 and 1839 the population of Holland
> grew 9.7 per cent
> Between 1839 and 1849 the population of Holland
> grew 6.9 per cent
> Between 1859 and 1869 the population of Holland
> grew 8.1 per cent
> Between 1869 and 1879 the population of Holland
> grew 12.0 per cent

Between 1849 and 1920 the Dutch population is said to have increased by 125 per cent; during the same period the industrial population grew 177 per cent, while the agricultural population grew only 94 per cent.[27] Even so the rural population grew more

---

[23] Baasch, *op. cit.*, p. 450.

[24] J. C. G. Evers, *Bijdrage Tot De Bevolkingsleer Van Nederland* ('s-Gravenhage, 1882), p. 4.

[25] I. J. Brugmans, *De Arbeidende Klasse In Nederland In De 19e Eeuw*, p. 140.

[26] Leonie Van Nierop, *De Bevolkingsbeweging Der Nederlandsche Stad* (Amsterdam, 1905), pp. 109 and 144.

[27] L. G. J. Verberne, *De Nederlandsche Arbeidersbeweging in De Negentiende Eeuw* (Amsterdam, 1940), p. 13. Brugmans reports the following changes in agricultural and industrial employment of the Dutch labor force:

rapidly than the urban population between 1813 and 1860. The outcome is attributable in part to the fact that in the early nineteenth century, the Dutch population underwent little urbanization.[28]

Although no figures are available respecting levels of employment in Holland during the nineteenth century, there is considerable evidence of unemployment in the first half of the century, particularly between 1840 and 1850. Apparently a population increment of 38 per cent between 1815 and 1850, during a period in which the level of economic activity in general was low in Holland, resulted in an excess supply of unskilled labor while at the same time there were shortages of skilled labor. The Dutch labor market was also characterized by immobility during the early nineteenth century. Wages were remarkably stable.[29] Unemployment, pauperism, and wages will be discussed in more detail in a later chapter.

An attempt has been made in this chapter to present a cursory sketch of the history of the Dutch economy and to indicate some economic circumstances which may have affected Dutch economic thinking and policy in the nineteenth century. A discussion of economic policy and governmental intervention with economic activities during the early nineteenth century has been reserved for the next chapter.

Total number of people employed in	Industry	Agriculture
1849	350,000	322,000
1859	372,000	253,000
1920	969,000	625,000

I. J. Brugmans, *De Arbeidende Klasse In Nederland In De 19e Eeuw*, p. 67. He does not give figures for other types of employment though data on the composition of the Dutch labor force are available for the year 1899 and periods thereafter. See I. J. Brugmans, "De Beroepstelling Van 1920 En Haar Voorgangsters," in *Welvaart en Historie.*

[28] Van Nierop, *op. cit.*, pp. 98 and 108; I. J. Brugmans, *De Arbeidende Klasse In Nederland In De Negentiende Eeuw*, p. 74.

[29] Brugmans, *ibid.*, pp. 140–141 and 152.

CHAPTER III

KING WILLEM I, VAN HOGENDORP, AND DUTCH ECONOMIC POLICY IN THE EARLY NINETEENTH CENTURY

In the present chapter we shall examine Dutch economic policy in the early nineteenth century together with the economic ideas of two non-academic figures, dominant on the Dutch scene at the time. The chapter will be centered around Willem I, King of the Netherlands from 1813 to 1840, and Gijsbert Karel Van Hogendorp, cabinet member from 1816 until 1825. Discussion of the actions and ways of thinking of these two figures will add to our historical perspective and understanding of the period. However, before the views of Willem I and Van Hogendorp are considered, a brief review of Dutch commercial policy during the eighteenth century will be required.

Though commercial and industrial interests at times conflicted in eighteenth century Holland, they are not easily distinguishable. Industries were often dominated by merchant capitalists while industrialists tended to invest surplus capital in commercial enterprises.[1] Industrial profits and expansion depended on export possibilities since the growth of the Dutch staple market had stimulated industrial production to a level in excess of what the domestic demand could absorb. The industrialists were usually aware of their dependence on foreign trade and at times made allowance for this dependence in their demands for protection. Yet they desired export duties on raw materials and import duties on competing foreign goods to protect their finished products. Often the above conflict was one of specific interests rather than

---

[1] H. R. C. Wright, *Free Trade And Protection In The Netherlands 1816–30* (Cambridge, 1955), p. 59.

commercial versus industrial interests; sometimes even the claims of different industrialists conflicted.[2]

The situation may be epitomized as follows. On the one hand there existed a natural kinship between industry and the free market; on the other hand there existed hostility between commercial interests and particular industries such as textiles. As the Dutch internal market began to decline, free trade became increasingly important to the merchants while industrialists, finding their export markets shrinking, intensified their demands for protection. The greater the impact of the decline of Holland's markets on her industry and commerce, the more urgent became the need for trade policy which could achieve a compromise between those favoring protection and those favoring expansion of external markets.

During most of the eighteenth century Holland was ruled by a merchant oligarchy, and for better of for worse, a coincidence of commercial interests and the government prevailed. A liberal tariff administered under the "Placaat" of 1725 remained in effect throughout most of the century, with duties of about 5 per cent on imports and exports. It was not until 1795, the time of Batavian rule, that many voices criticized favoritism to the commercial interests. Yet most proposals regarding modification of the tariff of 1725 were discarded. In 1810 Napoleon annexed the Kingdom of Holland for three years to follow, and in fact proceeded to amend the "Placaat" of 1725. Another achievement of French domination was the establishment of a centralized administration, which furnished Holland with the unifying influence it urgently needed. Conceivably the lack of unity during previous centuries had been a source of constraint on the expansion of the Dutch economy.[3]

When Willem I inherited the throne in 1813, after the regaining of Dutch independence, the merchants hoped once more to assert the supremacy of their interests. They would not give up their belief in the primacy of trade and persistently refused to recognize that new economic endeavors had to be discovered to replace

---

[2] *Ibid.*, p. 58.

[3] Treub blamed the absence of a national Dutch Industry in the nineteenth century on the weakness of mercantilistic policy during previous centuries. M. W. F. Treub, *Een Drietal Hoofdstukken Uit De Geschiedenis Der Staathuishoudkunde* (Haarlem, 1899), pp. 53–54.

activities which could no longer thrive now that European countries had undergone economic development. At the same time industrialists, particularly the Belgian industrialists, demanded protection against foreign manufactures, mainly those from Britain.[4] The drama of the old merchant-industrialist conflict now manifested itself in the two figures we are about to discuss. While Van Hogendorp represented the interests of the group which looked upon trade as the one and only source of Dutch prosperity, King Willem I realized the need for restructuring and reorientating of the Dutch economy.

THE ECONOMIC IDEAS OF WILLEM I
(1772–1843)

Willem I, who has been given such titles as the merchant King, the enlightened despot, or the neo-mercantilist, was the first Dutch ruler to design a national economic policy.[5] In 1813 this autocratic personality inherited the Napoleonic machinery, set up for the rule of a unified Holland during the French occupation, and began to develop this machinery under a napoleonic type of regime. He subscribed to the eighteenth century ideas of enlightenment and popular education, as demonstrated by his interest in the spreading of public education, his promotion of higher education, and his founding of the Academy of Sciences (Akademie van Wetenschappen). The King has been described as ahead of his time, at least in the sense of having a more mature view of the Dutch economy's future, and a wider range of ideas on welfare policy than his contemporaries.[6]

For the purpose of this study attention will be focused mainly on the King as a mercantilist, and upon the economic ideas which he carried out in his policies.[7] Though the King was not a theorist,

---

[4] Wright, *op. cit.*, pp. 99–101.

[5] Jan en Annie Romein, *Erflaters Van Onze Beschaving*, III (Amsterdam, 1939), 245; A. Goslinga, *Koning Willem I Als Verlicht Despoot* (Baarn, 1902); I. J. Brugmans, "Koning Willem I Als Neo-Mercantilist," in *Welvaart en Historie*, pp. 38–51.

[6] Z. W. Sneller, *Economische en Sociale Denkbeelden In Nederland In Den Aanvang Der Negentiende Eeuw (1814–1830)* (Haarlem, 1922), p. 11.

[7] The writer was unable to find any published works of the King, or any information concerning contact between the King and any Dutch or foreign economists who might have influenced his ideas.

his economic ideas were integrated and unified by the fact that they had to do primarily with the reconstruction and development of the Dutch economy. As Brugmans has stated, mercantilism has had a somewhat unique manifestation in each country because in the first instance it is expressed or supported by the apparatus of the state and because only secondarily is it theoretically founded. In general, therefore, mercantilism may be regarded as seeking a welfare policy of given content.[8] The most peculiar aspect of Willem I's mercantilism, as compared with the mercantilism that developed at different times in other countries, is the liberal strain with which it is imbued. This explains why I. J. Brugmans has termed the King's mercantilism as "a moderate or mitigated mercantilism, a mercantilism permeated with free trade elements." [9] At the same time the nineteenth-century King may be identified with other mercantilists of the seventeenth and eighteenth centuries in that he was striving for a unified economic policy, designed to enhance the economic well-being of the country.

It is important to recall that when Willem I came to power in 1813, the Dutch economy had been severely ravaged by a series of wars, which had followed a period of gradual decline of trade from 1730 onward. In 1814 the colonies were regained, but only after the British had thoroughly established trade relationships with the Indies. Dutch industries, in many cases founded upon Dutch commercial activities, were in distress around 1813. The national debt was great, taxes were burdensome, food prices high, and unemployment extensive. In addition, entrepreneurial spirit had been almost completely deadened.[10] Above all, the King was

---

[8] I. J. Brugmans, "Koning Willem I Als Neo-Mercantilist," *op. cit.*, p. 38.

[9] *Ibid.*, p. 50.

[10] W. M. F. Mansvelt, *Geschiedenis Van De Nederlandsche Handel-Maatschappij*, I, 13. Van Der Kooy provided illustrations of the conservatism and apathy of the nineteenth century Dutch businessmen. He reported that in 1824 a Dutch writer remarked that Holland's trade rested on surer foundations than England's because it depended on industrial products only to a slight extent whereas 70 per cent of the British exports were the products of industry. Van der Kooy, *op. cit.*, pp. 67–68. There was another species of Dutch merchants, Van Der Kooy reported, who vehemently opposed the development of Dutch transit trade in compensation for losses in the intermediary trade. Such were the Amsterdam merchants who in 1836 still considered a railway to Cologne unnecessary because their forefathers had desired no such speed and had welcomed the interruption of transport in the winter as an opportunity for making out accounts and balancing their books, and because merchants and storekeepers had no right to be in business unless they had enough

confronted with the task of restoring vitality in the various sectors of the Dutch economy. Among the tasks the King set for himself were the provision of support for industry, the re-establishment of trade relationships, the promotion of domestic investment, the creation of credit institutions, the reconstruction of colonial trade on a new basis.

Though mercantilistic elements had been part and parcel of Dutch commercial policy much more frequently than is usually admitted, Willem I was probably the first truly mercantilistic ruler of Holland.[11] The Dutch economy had not been unified prior to the nineteenth century; it had merely been subject to a multi-city and particularistic form of governmental organization and regulation. A consistent national economic policy could not, therefore, have been realized prior to the Napoleonic rule. In his capacity as Dutch ruler, Willem I was original in concentrating policy on the development of industry along side that of commerce, and above all on the development of the textile and metal indus-tries. Emphasis on industrial development thus gave unifying expression to the economic ideas of Willem I.[12]

Commercial policy under Willem I was relatively liberal in character. Though the tariffs enacted in 1816 and 1822 contained some moderately protective provisions, the import duties, relative to those found in European nations at the time, were compara-tively moderate.[13] Later on the King was swayed in a more protectionistic direction, mainly out of political consideration for the Belgian industrialists, but his commercial policy on the whole remained liberal. What marks the King's trade policy as mercan-

capital to practice the art of speculation and buy beyond immediate needs. Van Der Kooy, *op. cit.*, p. 80.

[11] The mercantilistic aspects of trade policy during earlier centuries were not usually conspicuous because the international-market position of Holland required commercial freedom. G. M. Verrijn Stuart described Dutch commercial policy prior to the nineteenth century as "free trade mercantilism." G. M. Verrijn Stuart, "Die Industriepolitik der Niederlaendischen Regierung," *Kieler Vortraege* gehalten im Institut fuer Weltwirtschaft an der Universitaet Kiel, 1936, p. 4.

[12] During his period of exile Willem I had lived in England and Prussia, where he had observed the industrial development of those nations. This experience is said to have been influential in the development of his economic ideas. *Nieuw Nederlandsch Biographisch Woordenboek*, edited by P. C. Molhuysen and P. J. Blok, I (Leiden, 1911), "Willem I," 1560–1566.

[13] N. W. Posthumus, *Documenten Betreffende De Buitenlandsche Handelspolitiek Van Nederland In De Negentiende Eeuw*, I, XVII. In 1813 the liberal "Placaat" of 1725 had been re-installed, however, with slight amendments of the period 1795–1810.

tilistic was his emphasis on the use of export duties and export restrictions to limit the outflow of raw materials and other products deemed essential to industrial advancement.[14]

It is consistent with mercantilistic policy to foster industry not only by means of trade policy and the granting of monopolistic privileges, but also by subsidization and by legislation designed to promote the consumption of domestic goods. Willem I instituted a "Fund of National Industry" (Fonds Van Nationale Nijverheid) in 1821, out of which to provide premiums or subsidies for the promotion of existing industries and for the creation of new industrial enterprises. The shipbuilding industry, for example, was subsidized out of this fund in 1830, as were the railroads. The King in person participated in a number of enterprises, attempting to stimulate private initiative by lending financial support. He also owned 4000 shares of the Netherland Trading Company, founded in 1824. In order to revive domestic textile industries he decreed in 1820 that all clothes and materials used by the army and navy, or in court, and all fabrics used for shipment to the colonies or by state-supported welfare institutions, were to be of domestic origin. His liberal tendencies, however, prevented his interfering with the consumption patterns of private citizens.

Willem I, aware of the flow of Dutch capital into foreign investments, assumed that the outflow retarded domestic economic development. Accordingly, for the purpose of promoting industrial development in Holland as well as for fiscal reasons, he had a law passed in 1816 under which the export of Dutch capital was restricted and regulated. The King also initiated road and harbour construction projects, the opening of numerous canals and new water connections, and even the beginning of a new railroad. Recognizing the important role which means of communication and transportation play in the economic development of a country, he utilized his abundant energy to stimulate this development and even financed it partly out of his own pocket.[15]

The King's views on the economic relationship between colonies and mother country were unusual when compared with the traditional view of the role of Dutch colonial enterprise. Instead of concentrating exclusively on the role of colonies as suppliers

[14] Brugmans, "Koning Willem I Als Neo-Mercantilist," *op. cit.*, p. 39.
[15] *Ibid.*, p. 44.

of raw materials and tropical goods, Willem I viewed the colonies as primarily export markets for the products of domestic industry. At the time when the colonies were returned to Holland in 1814, the Dutch East-India Company had already been dissolved, and private initiative for the development of trade relationships with the colonies was practically non-existent. As late as 1823, in fact, the Dutch, though burdened with the high costs of colonial administration, were not profiting through their colonies, because their products were inferior to British and American goods. Not even the differential import duties, which favored the importation of Dutch products into the colonies, sufficed to give Dutch merchants a good share of the colonial market.[16] The King thus had to concern himself with the colonial problem. He, therefore, introduced measures to revive colonial trade and these eventually culminated in his forming the Netherland Trading Company in 1824. In his dedication the company was described as "a strong and well-administrated institution which with sufficient capital and based on common effort was to give new life to everything." Its sphere of operation was to include all "that would promote trade, shipping, fishing, agriculture, and industry."[17]

The King utilized the Netherland Trading Company to carry out some of his economic policies, as well as to promote colonial commerce. Officially it was provided that the company's contracts with the colonies were to "concern only the buying, selling, delivery, and encouragement of goods and products" and were to "include no tendency towards monopoly, or the exclusion of the free trade of Netherlanders or of foreigners, or towards forced cultivation or forced deliveries."[18] In reality, however, the Company demonstrated great competence in the establishment and execution of monopolistic practices, managing to secure a sizable market for Belgian textiles, the need for which had previously been satisfied largely by British producers. The King was determined to derive benefits from the colonies by wiping out all detrimental foreign competition, with the Company serving as the intermediary organism between the state and the people with regard to colonial economic activities. The Company

---

[16] J. S. Furnivall, *Netherlands India* (Cambridge and New York, 1944), pp. 94–97.
[17] Mansvelt, *op. cit.*, pp. 66–68.
[18] Wright, *op. cit.*, p. 198.

was also to serve as examplar and to stimulate private entre-preneurship. Its overriding task, of course, was to develop the supposedly unlimited market possibilities existing in the colonies, and thereby to stimulate Dutch industry.

The King found it necessary to create various financial insti-tutions to supply his program with funds. In 1814 the Netherlands Bank was founded, in 1822 the Société Générale was established in Brussels to provide credit for Belgian industry, and in the same year the "Amortisatie Syndicaat," a sinking fund for the public debt was set up.[19] Whenever the King encountered obstacles to the carrying out of his plans, he approached it with a flexible state of mind and improvised tentative solutions.

What distinguished the King from most of his contemporaries was his realization of the urgency of the need to build up important Dutch export industries and with these to revive commercial activities generally. He believed the old intermediary trade, under which Holland had performed the function of carrier, stapler, and paymaster for Europe, to be out of date and incapable of great revival. Other solutions were needed. During much of his reign the Dutch economy was faced with serious unemployment, and the Dutch population itself seemed to be apathetic and lacking in entrepreneurial spirit. In the opinion of twentieth-century Mansvelt:[20]

What was chiefly lacking was the spirit of adventure, the courage to at-tempt great deeds and the power to sustain hardship and disappointment. ... We had been called the Chinese of Europe but we resembled the Chinese only in our conservatism; in industry and enterprise we resembled another ex-colonial power, the Portuguese. We had become a curiosity, a picturesque people in clogs and baggy breeches, and our only merchants were shopkeepers who sang behind the counter while waiting for their customers.

The King in effect sought to overcome this apathy and lack of enterprise. He excelled as a promoter and was eager to mobilize domestic capital and therewith to erect a national export indus-try, which would employ the paupers and evoke enthusiasm among potential entrepreneurs. Textiles offered such an oppor-

[19] A. M. De Jong, "The Origin and Foundation Of The Netherlands Bank," in *History of The Principal Public Banks*, collected by J. G. Van Dillen (The Hague, 1934), pp. 319–335. Mansvelt, *op. cit.*, pp. 26–30.
[20] Mansvelt, *op. cit.*, pp. 39–40. Quotation translated by Furnivall, *op. cit.*, p. 81.

tunity. After 1830 the first steps were taken towards the establishment of a textile industry in the Northern part of Holland. With the Netherland Trading Company serving as intermediary organ between colonial market outlets and Dutch manufacturers, the textile industry was founded on basis of a policy that fused economic and philanthropical considerations. The demand for textiles was assured by the Company, prices were determined by authority, and competition was entirely absent. However, by 1840 the artificially founded textile industry had directly created at least 14,600 employment opportunities, and by the 1850's after the state and the Company had ceased to intervene, the industry had developed to a level where it managed to compete successfully with foreign textile industries.[21]

Although Willem I failed to realize some of his fanciful hopes, his achievement must be regarded as quite instrumental in getting under way the industrial progress and commercial development which flourished in Holland during the latter half of the century. The King's ideas, as manifested in his approach to practical economic problems, represent an outlook and approach which evolved out of the particular historical-economic conditions found in late eighteenth- and early nineteenth-century Holland. We shall next turn to the economic views of Gijsbert Karel Van Hogendorp which were in sharp contrast to those of the King.

THE ECONOMIC IDEAS OF
GIJSBERT KAREL VAN HOGENDORP (1762–1834)

The ideas of Willem I concerning recovery of the Dutch economy were not shared by Van Hogendorp, who was Secretary of State and Cabinet Member in the government of the King in the period 1816 to 1825. This is evident in a number of his writings in which he presented his views about current economic problems; it is to be inferred also from the sources whence came some of his ideas and the foreign economists by whom he was influenced. Van Hogendorp's writings, which were quite numerous, represent a

[21] Mansvelt, op. cit., p. 340. For an elaborate treatment of the Netherland Trading Company and the Dutch textile industry see Mansvelt, op. cit., pp. 258–344. Also I. J. Brugmans, "Honderd Jaren Nederlandsche Nijverheid, 1830–1930," op. cit., pp. 119–123; Van Der Kooy, op. cit., pp. 74–76.

good proportion of the economic literature produced in Holland in the first quarter of the nineteenth century.[22] He was interested specifically in the application of principles of economics to the Dutch economy of his time, rather than in making contributions to economics per se. Beyond that he had a wide interest in the diffusion of economic ideas among the Dutch people. Discussion of Van Hogendorp's contributions serves a twofold purpose, therefore: (1) it shows how he differed from the King in his outlook on economic problems and policy measures, and (2) it reveals the foreign economic influences to which Van Hogendorp was subject, together with his relation to the academic economics of his time.

Van Hogendorp was born into an old Dutch regent family. His military training was obtained in the Prussian service, and he subsequently became officer in the Dutch army. In this capacity he came to the United States in 1783 where he became friendly with Thomas Jefferson. When he returned to Holland he began to study at the University of Leiden, because of disinterest in a military career. He received his doctoral degree of law in 1786. In 1787 he was appointed chief magistrate of Rotterdam, a position which he held until 1795 when he decided to go into business in Amsterdam. In 1813 he was appointed Secretary of State and Member of the Dutch cabinet.[23] In his economic writings Van Hogendorp always remained loyal to what he understood to be the merchant interests.

As stated before, the King and Van Hogendorp held sharply opposing views concerning the future of the Dutch economy. Whereas the King emphasized the importance of the industrial development of the country, Van Hogendorp insisted that the intermediary trading function of Holland must remain its main source of prosperity. As he proclaimed in 1813: "The sea is open, trade will revive ... the old times will return."[24] He regarded trade as peculiarly suited to the Dutch character and as a natural

---

[22] Otto Van Rees, *Verhandeling Over De Verdiensten Van Gijsbert Karel Van Hogendorp* (Utrecht, 1854), pp. 49 and 195.

[23] For biographical information on Van Hogendorp see: the previously cited study by Otto Van Rees, pp. 1–7; "Gijsbert Karel Van Hogendorp," in *Nieuw Nederlandsch Biographisch Woordenboek*, II, 587–593; Jan en Annie Romein, *Erflaters Van Onze Beschaving*, III, 207–244; K. E. Van der Mandele, *Het Liberalisme in Nederland* (Arnhem, 1933), pp. 9–27.

[24] *Brieven en Gedenkschriften van Gijsbert Karel Van Hogendorp*, edited by Mr. H. Graaf Van Hogendorp, IV ('s-Gravenhage, 1887), 236, Proclamatie, 17e November, 1813.

outgrowth of the location of Holland. In his opinion only those industries which were based on commercial activity had a chance to prosper. Artificial stimulation of factories and industrial enterprises, as contemplated by the King, could not succeed because Holland was only a small country and the development of her industries was conditioned by her export markets. Commercial freedom, if restored, would attract a large volume of trade to the Dutch, as it had in the good old times, and would give rise as well to a flourishing industry. In the tradition of the old Dutch commercial regents, Van Hogendorp blamed the failure of commercial recovery after 1813 on the protective aspects of commercial policy. Relying upon Adam Smith he continued that exports must be stimulated by means of free trade, sound competition, and low prices.[25]

Van Hogendorp was convinced that protective measures served only to favor inexperienced manufacturers who were unable to face foreign competition.[26] He claimed that the domestic manufacturers always held an advantage over the foreign manufacturer, in that the latter was burdened with additional costs of transportation, insurance, and import duties. If then the domestic producer still failed to produce at lower prices than the foreigner, governmental support of such an enterprise would be no benefit to the state or to the national well-being. Keeping high quality, cheap products out of the country in order to enforce the consumption of inferior, expensive, domestic goods was unjust and unreasonable. Under these circumstances it would be made possible for manufacturers to reject useful inventions and to continue automatically in their old routines, when they should be consulting the tastes of their consumers which undergo continuous change.[27]

Van Hogendorp also objected to the imposition of export duties on raw materials because he considered them unfair to the farmer, in that they lowered agricultural incomes. Legislation of this type, Van Hogendorp stated, was usually responsible for a diminution and deterioration in the production of raw materials, which in the end forced the manufacturers to import raw materials from foreign sources. It followed, according to Van Hogendorp, that a pro-

[25] Gijsbert Karel Van Hogendorp, *Bijdragen Tot De Huishouding Van Staat*, second edition by J. R. Thorbecke, I (Zalt-Bommel, 1854), 72.
[26] Van Hogendorp, *Bijdragen*, first edition, 1818–1825 ('s Gravenhage), V, 351.
[27] *Ibid.*, pp. 38 and 233–241.

tective policy had merely detrimental results and that low duties combined with free competition would optimize conditions for the development of industry.[28] Van Hogendorp also opposed giving protection to fishing and shipping industries as much as he opposed granting protection to agriculture. He pointed out that a high protective tariff was inconsistent with fiscal objectives. Experience had shown, he reported, that an increase in revenue would follow a lowering of the tariff. He concluded that public revenues could be increased only if Holland's national wealth increased.[29]

Some positive actions on the part of the government were permissible, however, Van Hogendorp believed. He described the following measures as purposeful and permissible: (1) spreading the knowledge of physics and technology and providing for the teaching of such subjects outside of universities and in the mother tongue; (2) advancement of the production of raw materials by means of contests and public exhibitions; (3) stimulation of domestic industries through encouragement of domestic consumption by the government, its employees, and the army and navy; (4) spreading information and publicizing statistical data; (5) construction and improvement of means of transportation, to the extent that it may not be achieved by private initiative; (6) maintenance of a sound currency system; and (7) prevention of begging and poverty.[30] Van Hogendorp agreed that the state should find work for the unemployed, but not by establishing governmentally-run enterprises which would cut into the market of private industry. He also believed in the income-effect of the tax burden, suggesting that the moderate taxation of necessities made for a greater supply of effort, and thus enhanced a nation's wealth.[31]

As far as Van Hogendorp was concerned, the primacy of trade for the Dutch economy was natural as well as self-evident, and he never ceased to equate the interests of commerce with the common

---

[28] *Ibid.*, VI, 428; I, 123; II, 146 and 178. Van Hogendorp justified protection of industry only in one special instance, namely when a product was subject to an excise tax. In this situation the domestic producer would be at a disadvantage in competing with foreigners if there were no import duty.

[29] *Ibid.*, I, 196 and 199.

[30] *Bijdragen*, first edition, I, 50–53; II, 79, 160–167; IV, 41, 93, 245; VIII, 410–428; IX, 78.

[31] *Ibid.*, IV, 93.

good. He did not recognize the importance of intervention to developing significant export industries and thereby to expand the Dutch economy. It was on this issue principally that Van Hogendorp differed from the King. Though the King was not as successful with his schemes for industrial development as he had hoped to be, in retrospect his diagnosis of Holland's economic future has been considered more realistic than Van Hogendorp's, which was based on the belief that the good old times and the Dutch trading monopoly could be restored.[32] It may be noted, however, that the free trade policies for which Van Hogendorp fought so vigorously were gradually adopted in the Netherlands after 1850. His trade policies have been described as premature by later Dutch economists; they are agreed that had a liberal policy been adopted in 1813, it would have led to further deterioration of the Dutch economy.[33]

As stated above, Van Hogendorp is of interest also, for the purpose of this study, because he was influenced by and interested in the work of foreign and Dutch economists, and because he maintained some contact with the academic economics of his time. As a result of his interest in the diffusion of economics in Holland, he encouraged the translation of foreign economic works into the Dutch language.[34] Van Hogendorp was in communication with the two leading academic economists of his time, H. W. Tydeman and Jan Ackersdijck, about economic questions.[35] As a matter of fact, Jan Ackersdijck, whose work will be discussed later, made use of Van Hogendorp's writings in his lectures on economics and statistics at the University of Utrecht.[36]

[32] Van Der Kooy, *op. cit.*, p. 104. Isaac Alexander Gogel, Minister of Finance and contemporary of Van Hogendorp, was as attached to laissez faire principles and as loyal to the commercial interests as was Van Hogendorp; but Gogel was concerned primarily with fiscal problems. See Jerome Alexander Sillem, *De Politieke en Staathuishoudkundige Werkzaamheid Van Isaac Alexander Gogel* (Amsterdam, 1864), pp. 142–143, 220–221, 269; and Van Rees, on Van Hogendorp, *op. cit.*, pp. 71–85, 154–155.

[33] K. E. Van Der Mandele, *Het Liberalisme in Nederland* (Arnhem, 1933), p. 72; Z. W. Sneller, *Economische Denkbeelden In Den Aanvang Der Negentiende Eeuw (1814–1830)*, p. 5.

[34] H. W. Tydeman, Introduction to the Dutch translation of Mrs. Marcet's *Conversations on Political Economy*, "Grondbeginselen Der Staats-Huishoudkunde" (Dordrecht, 1825).

[35] *Ibid.*, and W. C. Mees, "Eene Briefwisseling Tusschen Gijsbert Karel Van Hogendorp en Prof. Jan Ackersdijck," *Economisch-Historisch Jaarboek*, XII (1926), 100–124.

[36] *Ibid.*, pp. 107–108.

In Van Hogendorp's *Bijdragen* there are a great many references to foreign economists. His citations, however, were vague and sloppy as a rule; usually he did not devote more than a sentence or two to the views of any particular economist. The reader is left with the impression that Van Hogendorp cited foreign economists primarily in support of his own, liberal views on questions of economic policy. Because of the way in which he made reference to the economic ideas and writings of others it is not possible to determine the influence of specific foreign economists on Van Hogendorp's way of thinking.

Van Hogendorp announced the Dutch translation of Pietro Verri's *Meditazioni sulla Economia Politica* which had appeared in Holland in 1801 under the title of "De Staetkundige Oeconomie," in the preface of one of his own writings. It appears that Van Hogendorp added his own explanatory notes to the Dutch translation of Verri's work.[37] He recommended Verri's book very highly to the Dutch public and expressed general agreement with Verri's views on taxation. Van Hogendorp added the wish that more foreign economic literature of the same caliber be translated into the Dutch language.

Van Hogendorp made frequent reference to the French economists of his time. The names of Ganihl, Chaptal, C. Tempier, Louis Say, Jean Baptiste Say, Sully, and Sismondi are encountered several times in the ten volumes of his *Bijdragen*.[38] Van Hogendorp mentions these names either in connection with the development of the science of political economy in France, or because the cited economists elaborated on the advantages of adopting liberal trade policy in France. He considered J. B. Say's works the best in economics until Storch's *Cours d'économie politique* was published in Petersburg in 1815; the latter work, he said, could not be praised sufficiently.[39] In 1827, when the second edition of Sismondi's *Nouveaux Principes d'économie politique* was published, Van Hogendorp expressed deep admiration for ideas contained therein. He appreciated the realistic and practical nature of Sismondi's work as one of its main contributions, which according to him, made it superior to works of Britisch economists, who often

[37] Gijsbert Karel Van Hogendorp, *Gedagten Over 's Lands Finantien* (Amsterdam, 1802), Preface, p. VIII.
[38] *Bijdragen*, second edition, I, 56, 73, 74, 139; III, 59, 171; V, 63.
[39] *Ibid.*, III, 59; V, 62–63.

got lost in abstract concepts.[40] Van Hogendorp pointed out in his correspondence with Ackersdijck, that there were notable changes in the second edition of Sismondi's work, thus indicating that he had been familiar also with the first edition of the "Nouveaux Principes." Van Hogendorp agreed with Sismondi in advocating state intervention in the form of new legislation on behalf of the working class.

Van Hogendorp also credited Professor Kraus' academic lectures in Prussia and Von Hardenberg's economic reforms with having contributed to the diffusion of liberal economic ideas.[41] Though he was more favorably disposed toward French than English economists, Van Hogendorp was familiar with some of the British economic literature as well.[42] In his dissertation submitted at the University of Leiden in 1786 Van Hogendorp had made his first references to Adam Smith, specifically to his principles of taxation. Van Hogendorp cited Adam Smith frequently in his *Bijdragen;* in this work, however, Adam Smith's ideas were drawn into the discussion primarily to give support to arguments favoring free trade and competition.[43] A paragraph quoted from David Ricardo's *Proposals for an economical and secure currency,* 1816, is also found in the *Bijdragen.*[44] The entire paragraph is on the advantages of laissez faire. From the above cited correspondence between Van Hogendorp and Ackersdijck 1826–1828, it becomes evident that Van Hogendorp must also have been familiar with Ricardo's "Principles," since he addressed questions to Ackersdijck concerning Ricardian theory.[45] Apparently Van Hogendorp had difficulty understanding the writings of such British economists as Ricardo, McCulloch and McDonnell, for he was not convinced of the merit of Ricardo's and McCulloch's doctrines, not even after Ackersdijck had elaborated on the validity of the theories expounded by those economists.[46]

---

[40] W. C. Mees, "Eene Briefwisseling Tusschen Gijsbert Karel Van Hogendorp en Prof. Jan Ackersdijck," *op. cit.,* pp. 117–119.

[41] *Bijdragen,* second edition, V, 62.

[42] Van Rees pointed out that Van Hogendorp demonstrated a strong interest in British economic policy. Van Rees, on Van Hogendorp, *op. cit.,* p. 205.

[43] Otto Van Rees, "Het Collegie Van Adriaan Kluit Over De Statistiek Van Nederland," in *Tijdschrift Voor Staathuishoudkunde en Statistiek,* 12 (1855), 261. *Bijdragen,* second edition, I, 72; III, 196; V, 63; X, 361–362.

[44] *Ibid.,* I, 140.

[45] Mees, *op. cit.,* pp. 108–109.

[46] *Ibid.,* pp. 111–116.

Van Hogendorp also referred to Malthus' "famous work on population," but since he ignored the most important principles developed by Malthus in his "Essay," there is some doubt whether Van Hogendorp had actually read Malthus.[47] Certainly Van Hogendorp did not show much appreciation for the problems to which Malthus addressed himself; he was optimistic in regard to questions of overpopulation and poverty and felt assured that these problems could be relieved, in time, by education.[48]

Van Hogendorp was the first Dutch nineteenth-century writer on economic questions to support the liberal doctrines developed by French, British, and other foreign economists. He was well read in economic literature and showed an interest in the development of academic economics in Holland. In the courses taught by Jan Ackersdijck, Van Hogendorp's economic views were passed on to the Dutch students of economics. In view of the small number of writings of an economic nature then published in Holland, Van Hogendorp's works performed an important role in the spreading of information on economic issues, at that time. Van Hogendorp was primarily interested in justifying a liberal economic policy for the Dutch economy, one based upon liberal economic principles. Nevertheless, it must be remembered that through his influence on H. W. Tydeman and Jan Ackersdijck,[49] he also contributed to the diffusion of economic ideas in Holland during the early nineteenth century.

The views of King Willem I and Van Hogendorp were discussed in this chapter to show that the merchant-industrialist conflict of the eighteenth century continued during the early part of the nineteenth century. The views of these two figures, furthermore, represent two different outlooks respecting early nineteenth century economic conditions, economic prospects, and economic policies suited to Holland. The ideas of both Willem I and Van Hogendorp arose in part out of specifically Dutch economic circumstances, and subsequently entered into the context of nineteenth century Dutch academic economics.

[47] Van Rees, *op. cit.*, p. 203.
[48] *Bijdragen*, second edition, I, 150.
[49] Van Hogendorp had loaned his own copies of the works by McDonnell and Sismondi to Professor Ackersdijck, see Mees, *op. cit.*, and also had loaned his copy of one of the works by McCullogh to Professor H. W. Tydeman, see Introduction to the Dutch translation of Mrs. Marcet's *Conversations on Political Economy*, p. VIII.

CHAPTER IV

THE STRUCTURE
OF HIGHER EDUCATION IN HOLLAND
DURING THE NINETEENTH CENTURY

Since the development of academic economics is the dominant theme of this study, an examination of the structure of higher education in Holland during the nineteenth century is essential. Secondary education will be discussed only in the context of its direct relevance to the growth of economics. Considerations of the higher educational system in general will be limited to those variables which were most significant in relation to our subject matter. The first part of the chapter will include a discussion of deterrents to the development of economics, which will be followed by an examination of the gradual breakdown of these deterrents.

During most of the nineteenth century there were four universities in Holland; the State University of Leiden, founded in 1575; the State University of Groningen, founded in 1614; the State University of Utrecht, founded in 1636; and the Municipal University of Amsterdam, founded in 1632.[1] A fifth university, the Free Calvinist University of Amsterdam, was founded in 1880, and a Roman Catholic University in Nijmegen was founded in 1923.[2]

The Dutch universities are regulated by a constitutional law of higher education which introduces considerable inflexibility into the educational system.[3] The Dutch law of higher education,

[1] The Municipal University of Amsterdam actually has existed only since 1876. Before that it was considered an Athenaeum and did not have full university status. In this study it has been referred to as the University of Amsterdam even in respect to the period before it had been officially recognized as a university.

[2] *The World of Learning 1957*, Eighth Edition (London, Europa Publications Ltd., n. d.), pp. 625–630.

[3] See *Wetten, besluiten en beschikkingen betreffende Hoger Onderwijs En Wetenschappen*, edited by P. Van Werkum, Thirteenth Edition (Zwolle, 1954).

with all its amendments, specifies the number of faculties (departments) of a university, the number of professors to teach in each faculty, the subject requirements for students, the type of examinations which candidates for degrees are required to pass, the dates of the academic year and length of vacations, and the number of foreign students to be admitted, among many other details relevant to the functioning of universities. If changes are to take place in any aspect of the university system which is governed by law, the channels of constitutional amendment cannot be circumvented and consequently it is always a long and complicated process. This was also the case during the nineteenth century.

Of particular concern to this study are two aspects of the rigidity which characterized the Dutch university system during the first half of the nineteenth century and which hindered the development of economics, namely: (1) confinement to "the four faculties" which were to incorporate all branches of knowledge which were taught at Dutch universities, and (2) the requirement of Latin as the official university language. The four faculties permitted at Dutch universities were the following: the faculty of theology, the faculty of law, the faculty of medicine, and the faculty of philosophy. Apparently it was not until the law of higher education was revised in 1876 that a fifth faculty for natural sciences was introduced as a change in the structure of Dutch universities. The sixth faculty, which is the faculty of economics, was not legally acknowledged until 1937.[4]

The four-faculty structure of Dutch universities during most of the nineteenth century was not conducive to the growth of economics. In 1839 an article was published in one of the leading Dutch economic journals, expressing criticism of the pervasiveness of the old, four-faculty university structure. The author of the article explained that developments in the natural and political sciences had since long exposed the necessity of setting up additional faculties. Under the four-faculty structure, the author

[4] The School of Economics at Rotterdam was founded in 1913 and the economics faculty of the University of Amsterdam in 1921. However, it took 24 years after the founding of the Rotterdam School of Economics before the law of higher education was amended and the School was recognized as having equal status with universities. Degrees conferred by the Rotterdam School of Economics were not fully recognized until 1937. S. Elzinga, *Het Economisch Hoger Onderwijs Als Vertegenwoordiger Der Moderne Cultuur* (Wassenaar, 1941), pp. 1–2.

stated, such subjects as geography, economics and political science were pushed into a corner of the faculties of law and philosophy. As a result the above fields of knowledge became restricted and stultified because basically they did not fit into the faculty which united them with other disciplines.[5] Throughout the nineteenth century economics was an adjunct of the faculty of law of Dutch universities, and as such there was little scope for its development. The status of economics in the law faculties will be examined in more detail later in this chapter.

The other major impediment to the development of education in general and to economics in particular was the use of Latin as the official university language. It was not until 1855 that the board of trustees of universities became authorized to dismiss the Latin requirement for dissertations in subjects pertaining to courses which were lectured in the Dutch language.[6] Inaugural speeches were made in Latin until Professor Opzoomer broke the tradition in 1846. After 1859 it became conventional to present these orations in the native tongue.[7] During the first part of the nineteenth century Latin was maintained as the official lecturing language at the universities; however, it appears that this was not practiced at all faculties of universities.[8] It is not clear whether lecturing in Latin was required by law, or under rule set up by administrative bodies of the Dutch universities, or under the force of merely propagated tradition. Nor is it revealed in writings on the history of higher education in Holland at what precise date courses ceased to be presented in Latin.

Nineteenth century Dutch economists considered Latin to be inadequate as a medium of communication in economics, since the language did not supply the terminology needed to formulate concepts and ideas. Not of least importance was the fact that dissertations in economics, which in those days were representa-

---

[5] "De Vier Faculteiten," *Tijdschrift voor Staathuishoudkunde en Statistiek*, XVIII (1859), 407–427. The writer assumes that the article was written by the editor of the journal, B. W. A. E. Sloet Tot Oldhuis, though it was unsigned.

[6] *De Utrechtsche Universiteit*, II (1815–1936) (Utrecht, 1936), Chapter II, "De Utrechtsche Hoogeschool van 1815 tot 1877," by Dr. G. W. Kernkamp, p. 103, and *De Economist*, 9 (1860), 56, an article taken over from the *Algemeene Konst en Letterbode*.

[7] *De Utrechtsche Universiteit*, pp. 104–105.

[8] J. Huizinga, "Geschiedenis der universiteit gedurende de derde eeuw van haar bestaan, 1814–1914," in *Universiteit, Wetenschap, en Kunst*, in *Verzamelde Werken*, vol. VIII; also vol. I of *Academia Groninga*, p. 61. See also *De Economist*, 9 (1860), 56.

tive of the most significant literature in the field, would be limited to a select group of formally educated readers. The difficulty imposed on economics by the Latin requirement was experienced by W. C. Mees, one of the most prominent nineteenth century Dutch economists, who explained in the preface of his book on the "History of Banking in the Netherlands" that the study had originally been intended as a doctoral dissertation. The difficulties Mees encountered in rendering the subject in Latin forced him to relinquish it as a dissertation project, and he completed the study in the form of a book written in Dutch.[9] Simon Vissering also voiced his opinion on the inadequacy of Latin as a language for economics in his inaugural lecture held at the University of Leiden in 1850.[10]

Though the use of Latin may not have been required by the law of higher education,[11] breaking the convention and modernizing the educational process turned out to be an extremely difficult task. More than half the century passed by before Dutch was installed in all fields of higher education as the official language. The following reason may have motivated the Dutch to adhere to the use of Latin in higher education. Holland was a small country and the Dutch language had never been popular among foreign people in the sense that this was true of English, French, Spanish, Italian, or German. Ever since the foundation of Dutch universities, they had been dependent on an influx of foreign students and professors. Thus we learn from Huizinga that there were 16,557 foreign students besides 21,528 Dutch students at the University of Leiden between the years 1575–1700. More than half of the foreign students were of German nationality. At the University of Groningen, 27 out of 52 professors were German during the seventeenth century, while at Leiden and Utrecht about 1/6 of the total number of professors were of German nationality.[12] Though there

---

[9] W. C. Mees, *Proeve Eener Geschiedenis Van Het Bankwezen in Nederland* (Rotterdam, 1838), p. VIII. Mees wrote his dissertation shortly thereafter: *De vi mutatae in solutionem pecuniae debitae*, which dealt with the responsibilities of the debtor and the rights of the creditor when the exchange rates are altered during the time of a debt. See N. G. Pierson, "Levensbericht van Mr. W. C. Mees," in *Verspreide Economische Geschriften*, II (Haarlem, 1910), 330.

[10] Simon Vissering, "Over Vrijheid, Het Grondbeginsel Der Staathuishoudkunde," 1850, in *Verzamelde Geschriften*, II (Leiden, 1889), 142–143.

[11] *De Economist*, 9 (1860), 56.

[12] J. Huizinga, "Der Einfluss Deutschlands in der Geschichte der Niederländischen Kultur," in *Archiv für Kulturgeschichte*, XVI (Berlin, 1926), 213.

are no figures on the foreign component of Dutch universities during the nineteenth century, the Dutch may have wanted to maintain the academic-universal language in Holland for the sake of international exchanges of students and teachers. However, the perpetuation of Latin in the academic institutions of Holland could attract foreign students and professors only as long as Latin was maintained in other European universities as well. Though precise information is lacking it appears that Latin survived in the Dutch universities even after it had been dismissed by many of the institutions of higher learning in Western European countries.

We shall now turn to the movement away from the above deterrents and examine changes in the framework of academic economics in Holland. The emancipation of economics from the law faculties of universities did not take place until 1913 and will thus lead us beyond the period we are basically concerned with in this study. This is necessary if one is interested in the final outcome of gradual changes in the development of academic economics in Holland. In this chapter the establishment of separate economic faculties at universities and the founding of special institutions for higher education in economics will be discussed in spite of the fact that these are twentieth century developments.

As stated previously, economics in Holland remained an adjunct of the faculty of law of Dutch universities throughout the nineteenth century. This meant that economics was almost exclusively a subject for law students and taught by lawyers. In accordance with the law of higher education of 1876, all law students in Holland were to be examined in the principles of economics as part of a qualifying examination called "Kandidaatsexamen."[13] It was possible for law students to receive two doctoral degrees at that time, the second one a degree in political science ("Staatsweten-schappen"). If the student chose to work on the second doctoral degree, and apparantly there were only few who did, economics would also be part of the doctoral political science examination.[14] In 1921 the second doctoral degree for lawyers was eliminated but law students, as well as students at any other faculty, were

[13] J. Valkhoff, *Rechtssociologische Elementen In De Nederlandsche Rechtswetenschap Van De XIX De Eeuw* (Haarlem, 1955), p. 26.

[14] C. A. Verrijn Stuart, "Niederlande," in *Die Wirtschaftstheorie Der Gegenwart* (Wien, 1927), p. 142.

permitted to choose economics as an elective subject. Also the social geographers were required to study economics from then on.[15] This apparently had the effect of increasing the number of students who enrolled in economics courses.

But even coercion of students into economics courses was not likely to attract them permanently into the field of economics because of the type of courses offered. Normally there was one professor in the faculty of law entirely responsible for teaching all of economics and statistics. In many instances the professor was scheduled to teach several law subjects as well. It is evident that within this set-up a professor could rarely advance beyond the basic principles of economics as there was little scope for differentiation of the various fields of economics, and little opportunity for the professor to engage in scholarly work, besides his heavy teaching load. According to De Bosch Kemper, the law faculty of the University of Amsterdam consisted of only two professors from 1806 until 1862, when a third chair was added. Before 1862, when De Bosch Kemper taught there, he was responsible for teaching nine different subjects.[16] Since economics and statistics represented only two of those nine subjects, it follows that only limited time and attention would be devoted to them. The faculties of law at Utrecht and Groningen consisted of three professors since 1815, for the teaching of law, economics and statistics.[17]

Regarded from this angle it should not be surprising that the nineteenth-century academic program failed to produce a number of reputable economists. It was felt generally that the law students were not receptive to economics and only a small minority indicated an interest beyond the passing of required examinations.[18] As long as economics remained a subject auxiliary to law, in the described fashion, there was little chance for development of the discipline, or for an improved teaching program capable of at-

---

[15] *Ibid.* From 1815–1840 students of theology were required to study agricultural economics under the law of higher education. See D. S. Huizinga, "De Invloed Van Het Onderwijs En Van De Wetenschap Op Den Landbouw," in Z. W. Sneller, *Geschiedenis Van Den Nederlandschen Landbouw 1795–1940*, p. 236.

[16] J. De Bosch Kemper, *De Uitbreiding Van Het Hooger Onderwijs te Amsterdam* (1873), p. 11.

[17] J. Huizinga, *Verzamelde Werken*, VIII, 64.

[18] H. Van Der Vegte, "De Staathuishoudkunde in het Kader van het Hooger Onderwijs," in *Sociaal-Economische Opstellen Aangeboden Aan Mr. H. B. Greven* (Haarlem, 1916), p. 382.

tracting students and evoking interest in the study of economic problems.

Such was the situation until 1913 with one exception, that of the Technical School in Delft (Polytechnische School te Delft), which was primarily a school for engineers and was founded in 1842. The Technical School was an institute of secondary education and one of the very few institutions which offered economics at that level of education. In 1905 the Technical School of Delft was converted into an institution of higher education, and it was here that the first chair was created for economics per se, and not as belonging to a law faculty.[19] C. A. Verrijn Stuart was the first professor to occupy this chair in 1906; in 1909 a second chair was added (an extraordinarius) for the teaching of business economics.[20] In all other cases before 1913, economics had been taught from chairs founded in law faculties, which were not set up for economics but which included economics and statistics among several law subjects, political history, or other related subjects comprised by the law faculty.

The emancipation of economics as an independent discipline may be considered to have taken place in 1913. However, it is only in an indirect way that the founding of the School of Economics in Rotterdam symbolized the addition of a sixth faculty, a faculty of economics in the university system. Three forces operated against the establishment of a separate training program in economics: (1) opposition from business circles in which it was held that trade was a practical endeavor and not a science for which young men could be prepared in the classroom; (2) opposition from the state, which was unwilling to lend financial support to the establishment of a separate program for education in economics; and (3) resistance by administrators of the institutions of higher education, who were reluctant to modify tradition by adding a new faculty to the university structure.[21] On the other hand, there was a certain amount of awareness of the fact that a business training would probably turn out more competent individuals for positions in business and industry than those men only

[19] *Wetten, besluiten en beschikkingen betreffende Hooger Onderwijs en Wetenschappen*, p. 29.

[20] N. J. Polak, "Het Economisch Hooger Onderwijs". in *Verspreide Geschriften*, II (Purmerend, 1933), 490.

[21] S. Elzinga, *op. cit.*, pp. 25 and 45.

exposed to practical experience.[22] Also there were government positions and diplomatic services for which no adequate training program had been provided in Holland. This realization grew with the establishment of business education programs in neighbouring countries, which attracted the Dutch students to foreign institutions. It became customary for young men in Holland, who planned a business career, to enroll in business schools (Handels Hoogescholen) in other countries such as Belgium, Austria or Germany.

This concern about keeping up with developments in other countries was not confined to business circles, but was shared by the government as well. In 1842 the government assigned D. Buddingh to translate a work by C. F. Nebenius, written in German, "Ideas concerning the promotion of Industry by means of higher education."[23] The same Mr. Buddingh was also held responsible for a survey of industrial and commercial institutions in Europe which he published under the title of "Industrial and Business Academies and other educational institutions for the promotion of industry and trade in Europe."[24] This survey was conducted the same year in which the founding of the Polytechnische School at Delft took place, in 1842. The survey indicated the degree of backwardness of the Dutch educational system regarding the preparation of students for the business world, when compared to other countries. No remedial action was taken during the next 67 years until the same question demanded attention in 1909 when the government sponsored Mr. Everwijn to examine business schools in Germany and in Austria-Hungary.[25]

[22] In 1845 Dr. S. Sarphati had founded an organization for training in commerce and industry (Inrichting voor onderwijs in koophandel en nijverheid), which gave rise to the first Business School (Openbare Handelschool) of Amsterdam in 1846. Professors from the Municipal University were to teach at this school but unfortunately it was discontinued in 1850 because there was a lack of students and financial support. Thus the Dutch attempts at a business education program during the nineteenth century were always intimately related to the teaching of economics. See N. W. Posthumus, "De Faculteit Der Handelswetenschappen," in *Gedenkboek Van Het Athenaeum En De Universiteit Van Amsterdam 1632–1932* (Amsterdam, 1932), 354.

[23] C. F. Nebenius, *Denkbeelden Nopens De Bevordering Van Nijverheid Door Onderwijs*, Uit het Hoogduitsch door D. Buddingh ('s Gravenhage, 1842).

[24] D. Buddingh, *Over Industrie en Handels Akademieen En Verdere Inrigtingen van Onderwijs Ter Bevordering Van Nijverheid en Handel in Europa* (Amsterdam and Delft, 1842).

[25] Mr. Everwijn, "Handelshoogescholen in Duitschland en Oostenrijk-Hongarije," *Verslagen en Mededeelingen* van de Afdeeling Handel van het Departement van Landbouw, Nijverheid, en Handel (Jaargang, 1909), no. 1.

Apparently the academic economists (i.e., lawyers who taught economics at the law faculties of universities) played only a minor role in bringing about the emancipation of economics. It was purely with the incentive of private businessmen and predominantly on the basis of private financial support that the School of Economics at Rotterdam was founded in 1913. At first the school was set up to offer a two-year training program in preparation for business positions, jobs with Chambers of Commerce or trade unions, secondary education teaching positions or diplomatic and accounting services.[26] In fact, originally the school was named Business School (Handels-Hoogeschool). Though a more extensive program terminating with a doctoral degree in economics was intended it was not offered right away. Almost 25 years elapsed before the higher education program of the Business School of Rotterdam received lawful recognition, but long before 1937 the doctoral program had been instituted. The curriculum, which when it was first developed emphasized business education and such subjects as bookkeeping, business arithmetic, modern languages and business correspondance, underwent considerable modification and was transformed into a curriculum which concentrated on economics. The first 25 years were crucial to the development of the institution and in 1938 its name change from Business School to School of Economics symbolized its process of maturation.

The enrollment of the School of Economics at Rotterdam was encouraging from the start. During the year 1913–1914 the students numbered 70 and in the following year the number of students rose to 138, 96 of whom represented newly enrolled students.[27] In 1920 the enrollment was up to 550 students and the school continued to expand until a Faculty of Business was set up at the University of Amsterdam in 1922.[28] However, the total number of economics students in Rotterdam and Amsterdam continued to rise, so that in 1927 a third, Roman Catholic School of Business, was established in Tilburg. In 1938, one year after the legal recognition of the doctoral program in economics, a total number of 779 students had passed their doctoral examinations

[26] Elzinga, *op. cit.*, p. 49.
[27] Polak, *op. cit.*, p. 490.
[28] Elzinga, *op. cit.*, p. 49.

and 136 had received Ph. D. degrees at the three institutions (Rotterdam: 559 doctoral candidates and 129 Ph. D. degrees; Amsterdam: 148 and 6; Tilburg: 72 and 1 respectively).[29] Under the law of higher education of 1937 all three names were changed respectively from Business School to School of Economics and from Faculty of Business to Faculty of Economics, and the two Schools of Economics were considered to have equal status as the university faculty of economics.[30]

The founding of the School of Economics at Rotterdam in 1913 in spite of its initial orientation toward business training, probably represented the most significant formal step toward the development of economics as a separate field of investigation. It is interesting to note that mainly a group of businessmen were responsible for the coming into existence of the school.[31] The striving for establishment of a business faculty at the University of Amsterdam also came from non-university circles.[32] Peculiarly enough, when the Business Faculty was instituted in 1922, it demonstrated a pronounced trade-school orientation rather than an academic training program.[33] However, the faculty underwent rapid reform along similar lines as the School of Economics at Rotterdam, and expanded increasingly in the academic direction.[34]

The above discussion of the academic framework of economics during the nineteenth century was intended to throw light on the nature and development of Dutch economic thought during the same period. Economics was subjected to serious constraints within the academic structure then prevailing. As long as it was denied an independent existence and had to comply with the

---

[29] Polak, *op. cit.*, p. 493.

[30] *Wetten, besluiten en beschikkingen betreffende Hoger Onderwijs en Wetenschappen,* p. 113.

[31] Z. W. Sneller, Rede Uitgesproken Ter Gelegenheid Van De Herdenking Op 8 November 1938, Van De Stichting Der Nederlandsche Handels-Hoogeschool, Hoogeschool Voor Economische Wetenschappen, p. 10; Polak, *op. cit.*, p. 490, and Elzinga, *op. cit.*, p. 48.

[32] Th. Limperg Jr., "De Faculteit der Economische Wetenschappen der Universiteit van Amsterdam," Rede uitgesproken ter gelegenheid van haar Vijfentwintig Jarig Bestaan door haar Voorzitter, Overdruk van het *Jaarboek der Universiteit,* 1946/47, p. 2.

[33] *Ibid.*, pp. 5–6.

[34] At the University of Leiden, Utrecht, Groningen, and at the Roman Catholic University at Nijmegen, economics at present is still taught in the faculty of law exclusively. The Municipal University of Amsterdam, as stated above, has a faculty of economics and the Free Calvinist University of Amsterdam has a faculty of economics and social science.

conventions, practices and boundaries of a totally different discipline, the prospects for the development of economics were not favorable. After all, there were no faculties of economics, nor were there teachers exclusively devoted to economics (not to mention the possibility of specialization within economics), nor was it possible for students to study economics per se. The academic scene thus clarifies the type of education to which the Dutch economists of the nineteenth century were exposed. A group of representative Dutch nineteenth-century economists will be investigated subsequently.

CHAPTER V

THE HUMAN CONTEXT OF THE DEVELOPMENT OF ECONOMICS

In a study of the development of economic thought some attention must be focused on economists as such and upon the impact of their functions on society as well as upon the progress of the discipline. Furthermore, since certain socio-cultural and institutional factors constitute a part of the milieu of a science, the discipline should also be examined in terms of the human setting in which it develops. The human representatives of a field of knowledge play a role in the development of this discipline to the extent that they act upon it. Regarded from this angle economics in Holland during the nineteenth century was influenced through a variety of different capacities in which economists engaged. It is to be assumed that the educational background as well as the particular career pursued by an individual influences his attitudes toward economic problems and toward the body of economic knowledge. All these biographical factors lumped together may be described as the human context of economics.

Discussion in this chapter will be centered upon the Dutch economists of the selected period, with concentration on the relationship of each particular individual to economics rather than on the nature of his specific contribution. A representative group of economists has been selected on the basis of their connections with academic economics either in educational or literary capacities. Minor figures are ignored in this chapter. The economists selected for discussion have been chosen because their life histories illustrate the career patterns of Dutch economists in the nineteenth century and illuminate the human context in which Dutch economics was developed and applied.[1]

This chapter is divided into two parts. Part I, "Academic Economists," is devoted to academic economists: to their educational backgrounds, their careers, their extra-curricular activities, and, in some cases, to careers pursued outside the academic world. Part II, "Contributors Who Were Not Economists," deals with several figures who made contributions to the development of economics in Holland, even though they were not economists by profession. Emphasis is upon activities centered around the economic discipline rather than upon the content and quality of academic economics. Relevant non-economic activities engaged in by economists will also be considered, but only insofar as they are significant elements of the human context.

ACADEMIC ECONOMISTS

Economists in the Teaching Profession

An academic economist, as defined for the purpose of this study, is any person who for a considerable part of his life was involved in one or more activities directly related to the use or the development of economics as a body of knowledge. This definition thus includes economists who worked outside as well as those who worked within the system of higher education. The latter group shall be turned to first and will be discussed in terms of (1) activities which preceded their academic career; (2) activities which constituted their academic career; and (3) activities which were extra-curricular to their academic career.

As noted in Chapter IV, the Dutch system of higher education during the nineteenth century did not offer training for economists per se. All economists under consideration here had received advanced degrees in the field of law. After 1815 students of law at all Dutch universities were required to take a course in eco-

---

[1] A substantial amount of biographical information has been obtained from the *Nieuw Nederlandsch Biographisch Woordenboek*, edited by C. P. Molhuysen, P. J.Blok, *et al.* (Leiden, 1911–1937), 10 volumes. This biographical dictionary will be referred to in this chapter as *N. N. B. W.* with the particular volume number and pages relevant to the person under discussion.

[2] Otto Van Rees, "Het Collegie Van Adriaan Kluit Over De Statistiek Van Neder-

nomics and statistics.[2] The training in economics and statistics, however, represented only an insignificant portion of the total law curriculum. In some instances a law student became inspired by the professor teaching economics and continued to develop his interests in that field. Occasionally a student was motivated to write a dissertation on a subject in the field of economics. However, until the Latin requirement for dissertations was discontinued around the middle of the century, dissertations in the field of economics met with considerable difficulties. Thus even the students who were inclined to delve into economic problems had little opportunity to do so during the years of their formal education.

Nineteenth-century Dutch economists received an advanced training in the law faculty of the universities and usually started their professional careers as practicing lawyers. The length of the early law career of these economists varied, depending on the success of the individual as a lawyer and upon the availability of alternative positions. Some of the economists switched from law to journalism, or attempted to combine the two professions. The time between the termination of legal studies and the beginning of a teaching career in economics varied with individuals from three to twenty-two years (see chart.) In some cases a lawyer initially established a reputation as economist by means of submission of a prize essay on an economic issue. Usually the subject had been selected by a learned society or a university board and was promoted in the form of a prize winning contest. In some instances only a single essay was submitted while at other times there were several from which the most outstanding essay had to be selected. The writer of the best essay received a prize as well as considerable publicity. Usually the winner also received one or more invitations to membership in academies or learned societies. Publicity based on a prize winning essay may well have increased a candidate's eligibility for university teaching positions.

It was not uncommon for a man to receive a professorship at the university from which he had also received his doctoral degree. When a person was appointed to a teaching position in economics at a university he always occupied a chair in the law faculty, as

land," *op. cit.*, p. 248. S. Vissering has stated that the requirement for the teaching of statistics to law students applied to the University of Leiden alone, at first. Gradually, however, it spread to the other law faculties in the country. S. Vissering, "De Statistiek Aan De Hoogeschool," *De Gids* (1877), No. 11, p. 1.

CHART I

	KLUIT (1735–1806)	TYDEMAN (1778–1863)	ACKERSDIJCK (1790–1861)	MEES (1813–1884)
I. PRE-ACADEMIC				
Degree: date	1762	1799	1810	1838
University	Utrecht	Leiden	Utrecht	Utrecht
Age	27	21	20	25
Initial Career	Teacher, Dean of Latin schools	Lawyer, Teacher at Academies	Lawyer, Teacher at Luik, Academie	Lawyer, Secret. Chamb. of Commerce Rotterdam, 1843
Prize Essays		Wrote at least 7 prize essays 1807–1821		
II. ACADEMIC				
Institution	Leiden	Leiden	Utrecht	Second. school, Rotterdam. 1845
Date	1778	1812	1831	
Age	43	34	41	32
No. yrs. between degree & teaching	16	3	15	7 Econ.
Subjects taught	Econ., Statist., History, Diplomacy, Medieval Hist.	Econ., Statist., Encyclopaedie, History of Law, Commercial Law.	Econ., Statist., Pol., History, Government.	
No. years taught	1778–1806 = 28	1802–1848 = 46	1825–1860 = 35	1
III. EXTRA-CURRICULAR				
Translations		Marcet; Marcet; Senior; Von Schroeder; Alison		
Journals		Founded "Magazine of Pauperism" 1817–	Founder Journal on Colonies, 1844–1847	

Statistics		Chairm. of Nat. Com. f. Statist. 1859–1860 Memb. Union f. Statist.	Com. on Currency, 1855 and 1872
Gov. Commissions		Com. f. Regulation of Higher Educ. 1828	
Political		Municip. Council Utrecht Provincial State 1851	
Learned Societies	Utrecht. Genoot. 1801 Maatsch. d. Nederl. Letterk. 1804 Zeeuwsch Genoot. 1807 Koninkl. Inst. v. Wetensch. 1809 Maatsch. v. Wetensch. (Haarlem) 1812 Maatsch. "Felix Meritis" 1819 Leidsch. Maatsch. v. Letterk.	Koninkl. Akad. v. Wetensch. Maatsch. d. Nederl. Letterk.	Maatsch. "Felix Meritis" Koninkl. Akad. v. Wetensch. 1858 Maatsch. Nederl. Letterk. Honorary Mem. Cobden Club
IV. NON-ACADEMIC CAREERS			
Banking			Secret. Netherl. Bank, 1849–1863 President Netherl. Bank, 1863–1884
Political			

CHART I (continued)

	VAN REES (1825–1868)	VISSERING (1818–1888)	DE BRUYN KOPS (1822–1887)	SLOET TOT OLDHUIS (1808–1884)
I. PRE-ACADEMIC				
Degree: date	1851	1842	1847	1836
University	Utrecht	Leiden	Leiden	Utrecht
Age	26	24	24	28
Initial Career	Lawyer	Lawyer, Journalist	Lawyer, Dept. of Finance	Burgomaster Lawyer
Prize Essays	On Van Hogendorp, 1854			
II. ACADEMIC				
Institution	Groningen: 1858 Utrecht: 1860	Leiden	Second. school Delft	
Age	33	32	42	
Date	1858	1850	1864	
No. years between degree & teaching	7	8	17	
Subjects taught	Econ., Statist., Gov. Law, Common Law, Polit., Hist.,	Econ., Statist., Polit., Hist.,	Econ.	
No. years taught	1858—1868=10	1850—1879=29	1864—1868=4	
III. EXTRA-CURRICULAR				
Translations				Dumont; Droz; Martineau; Roscher
Journals	Founded Pantheon 1853–1858	Editor of De Gids: 40 yrs.	Founded De Economist, 1852—	Founded Tijdschr. v. Staathuishoudk. en Statist 1841–1875

	1858–1868	1850–1861 Union f. Statist. 1849–1876	of Union f. Statist.	
Gov. Commissions		Com. f. Currency Com. f. Examinations f. Diplomats	Dept. of Finance 1851–1860 Com. f. Railroads Com. f. Currency	
Political	Municip. Council Utrecht 1855–1858	Minister of Finance, 1879–1881		
Learned Societies	Maatsch. "Felix Meritis" Koninkl. Akad. v. Wetensch. 1866 Prov. Utrechtsch Genoot. v. Kunst & Wetensch. Maatsch. Nederl. Letterk.	Koninkl. Akad. v. Wetensch. Maatsch. d. Nederl. Letterk.	Maatsch. d. Nederl. Letterk.	
IV. NON-ACADEMIC CAREERS				
Banking				
Political			Mem. Second Chmbr. 1868–1881 Chairm. part of time	Municip. Council Provinc. State Second Chambr. 1848–1860 Double Chambr. 1840, 1848

CHART I (*continued*)

	DEN TEX (1795–1854)	DE BOSCH KEMPER (1808–1876)	BUYS (1826–1893)
I. PRE-ACADEMIC			
Degree: date	1817	1830	1850
University	Utrecht	Leiden	Utrecht
Age	22	22	24
Initial Career	Lawyer	Lawyer	Lawyer Journalist
Prize Essays		Geschiedkundig Onderzoek Naar de Armoede, 1851	
II. ACADEMIC			
Institution	Amsterdam	Amsterdam	Amsterdam-Leiden
Age	25	44	36
Date	1820	1852	1862
No. years betw. degree & teaching	3	22	12
Subjects taught	Econ. Statist. Natural Law Common Law Civil Law	Econ. Statist. Encyclopaedie Criminal Law Gov. Law Common Law Political Hist.	Econ. Statist. Gov. Law Criminal Law Common Law
No years taught	1820—1852 = 32	1852—1862 = 10	1862—1893 = 31
III. EXTRA-CURRICULAR			
Translations			
Journals	Founded "Contribu-	Founded *Jaarb. v.*	

Statistics		Co-founder of Union f. Statist. 1848	
Gov. commissions			Staatscom. en College v. Visscherijen
Political	Second Chambr. 1842–1847 Double Chambr. 1848	Municip. Council Amsterdam Provincial State N.-Holland Mem. Second Chambr. 1867	
Learned Societies	Maatsch. d. Nederl. Letterk.	Maatsch. d. Nederl. Letterk.	Maatsch. "Felix Meritis" Koninkl. Akad. d. Wetensch.
IV. NON-ACADEMIC CAREERS			
Banking			
Political			

this represented the only opportunity for the teaching of economics in the higher educational system of Holland at that time. It is to be recalled that during the nineteenth century only one member of each Dutch law faculty was engaged to teach ecomics. The economist was responsible for transmitting all the knowledge of economics and statistics which students were expected to obtain, and in addition he was involved with the teaching of law courses.

Throughout most of the nineteenth century economics and statistics were coupled as university courses and were always taught by the same professor. Precise information about the content of economics and statistics courses is lacking, so that there is some doubt whether the two subjects were always divided up into separate courses. The first person who ever taught statistics to law students in Holland was Adriaan Kluit (1735–1806), who became professor of history at the University of Leiden in 1778.[3] After his introduction of statistics into the university curriculum, around 1802, had duly impressed the authorities, he received the title of "Professor Antiquit. et Historiae Imprimis Diplomaticae, Nec Non Statistices Regni Hollandici" in 1806.[4] Kluit, however, was a statistician in the tradition of Achenwall, who regarded statistics as a descriptive narrative about the state with an account of all its resources, institutions, potentialities, and pecularities.[5] This approach to statistics had little resemblance to the purpose and method of the numerical science which eventually became identified with the term of statistics. As a matter of fact, Kluit failed to make a distinction between economics and statistics, as the title of one of his manuscripts indicates: "Voorlezingen over de Statistiek of Staathuishoudkunde der Vereenigde Nederlanden, in het Koningrijk Holland."[6] Thus early in the nineteenth century the teaching of statistics in Holland consisted of a descriptive account of one or more countries in terms of a variety of characteristics relevant to policy formation.

Jan Ackersdijck (1790–1861), according to a report of one of his students,[7] treated economics and statistics as two individual

---

[3] *N. N. B. W.*, III, 696–698.

[4] *Algemeene Konst En Letter-Bode*, II (1806), No. 44 (31 October, 1806), 273.

[5] S. Vissering, "De Statistiek Aan De Hoogeschool," *op. cit.*, p. 2.

[6] Van Rees, *op. cit.*, p. 248.

[7] B. W. A. E. Sloet Tot Oldhuis, "Mr. J. Ackersdijck," *Tijdschrift Voor Staathuishoudkunde en Statistiek*, XXI (1861), 169–185.

subjects. The statistics course was split into (1) statistics, and (2) the theory of statistics. The former part, statistics, was sub-divided into (a) general statistics and (b) particular statistics. The heading of particular statistics was assigned by Ackersdijck to the statistics of Holland. In his lectures about general statistics Ackersdijck dealt with the stages of development of different peoples throughout the world, comparative statistics of different countries with respect to size, resources, climate, and location. Apparently he developed population theory quite extensively in connection with such factors as education, religion, culture, and means of subsistence. Ackersdijck is said to have considered himself a follower of Malthus.[8]

Otto Van Rees (1825–1868), who was a student of Ackersdijck, taught statistics in a manner very similar to that of his teacher. It seems that he concentrated primarily on the colonies and on taxes, when dealing with statistics pertaining to the Netherlands.[9]

There is no further information available about statistics courses in Holland in the nineteenth century. Eventually the subject of statistics outgrew its descriptive stage and developed into the type of field known as statistics today, taught by a person with specialized training.[10] However, when this change of orientation in statistics took place and which agents were responsible for its development in Holland are factors which have remained unknown.

Information about the content of economics courses taught in those days is almost equally scarce. The only details available about courses in economics refer to those taught by Ackersdijck and Van Rees, who seem to have been unusually popular teachers. Ackersdijck divided his course into four sections and dealt with the origin, the circulation, the distribution, and the consumption of wealth. Emphasis was placed on the application of theories to specifically Dutch economic problems.[11] Van Rees was influenced by Ackersdijck also in his approach to the teaching of economics. In 1861 Van Rees published a booklet, *Overzigt der Staathuishoud-*

[8] Otto Van Rees, "De Wetenschappelijke Werkzaamheid van Mr. J. Ackersdijck," *Utrechtsche Studenten-Almanak* (Utrecht, 1862), pp. 169–212.

[9] J. A. Fruin, "Levensbericht van Mr. Otto Van Rees," *Levensberichten Der Af-gestorvene medeleden van de Maatschappij der Nederlandsche Letterkunde* (1869), p.146.

[10] Anthony Beaujon (1853–1890), for example, became professor of statistics at the Athenaeum of Amsterdam in 1884 and at the same time he was director of the Statistical Institute of the Athenaeum. *N. N. B. W.*, X, 35–36.

[11] Van Rees, on Ackersdijck, *op. cit.*, p. 186.

kunde (overview of Economics), which served as an outline for the teaching of an economics course. It was re-edited several times and was probably used by other teachers of the subject as well. In most of his writings Van Rees concentrated on economic history and the history of economic thought, and one would suspect that his strong historical interests also carried over into his teaching. As one of his students has reported, Van Rees preferred to examine practical issues, in his courses, and he studied these issues always from a historical viewpoint. It was his conviction that without precise knowledge of reality, the application of theory would be fruitless.[12]

Besides Ackersdijck and Van Rees the most influential teacher of economics was Simon Vissering (1818–1888), who attracted and guided many students during the twenty-nine years of his teaching career at the University of Leiden. In 1860 he published a handbook of economics, *Handboek Van Praktische Staathuishoudkunde*, which was re-edited three times between 1860 and 1878.[13] The title of this work, *Handbook of Practical Economics*, supplies a hint about Vissering's orientation regarding the teaching of economics. His book was divided into three parts: (1) Production in the economy; (2) Welfare in the economy; and (3) Economics of the state. The treatment of these three areas of economics was centered around actual problems and institutions. Part I, for example, included a discussion of industrial activity in the economy with respect to protection, problems of monopoly, and intervention by the state. Part I also included an examination of the colonies, the monetary system, and banking and credit institutions. Part II was devoted to the population question, to causes of and ways of dealing with poverty, and to wages, wealth, and property. In Part III Vissering addressed himself exclusively to the area of

---

[12] Fruin, *op. cit.*, p. 128.

[13] Another very popular Dutch textbook was J. L. De Bruyn Kops' *Beginselen Van Staathuishoudkunde* (Principles of Economics) (Amsterdam, 1850). Although the teaching career of De Bruyn Kops was a very short one, his work on "Principles," which was the first Dutch textbook in economics, had a significant impact on the teaching of economics in Holland. This work presented a more popular treatment of basic economics than Vissering's book and went through five editions between 1850 and 1873. According to N. G. Pierson all Dutch students of economics during the third quarter of the nineteenth century were indebted to De Bruyn Kops, for all began their studies with his book on "Principles." Quoted by J. K. W. Quarles Van Ufford, "Levensberichten van Mr. Jacob Leonard De Bruyn Kops," in *Levensberichten Der Afgestorven Medeleden Van De Maatschappij der Nederlandsche Letterkunde* (Leiden, 1889), p. 50.

public finance. By means of this handbook Vissering was able to communicate with an audience which extended beyond the law students of the University of Leiden, as he enlightened the Dutch public about the practical relevance of economic questions. Other than Vissering's textbook we have no evidence regarding the way he went about teaching economics.

In general it is known that each professor of economics offered only a single economics course, and it is not clear whether the course was varied from year to year. On the other hand, it is known that an economist who occupied a chair at a law faculty was normally required to teach from two to six subjects in addition to courses in economics and statistics (see chart., page 48). Not all of these subjects were taught during each year, but nevertheless the efforts of the professor had to be spread over all these areas. When regarded from this angle it seems that only limited allowance was made for intensive study by the professor in preparation for the teaching of each individual course.

Despite the heavy teaching load which appears to have been customary for Dutch university professors, most of them were involved also in a number of extra-curricular activities. The type of activities considered here include: the translation of foreign economic literature, the founding and editing of economic journals, the serving on governmental committees for the study of economic problems, the serving in setting up of statistical organizations, and the functioning in municipal, provincial, or national governments. This list, of course, does not apply to each professor under consideration. However, it will be relevant to consider briefly the variety of capacities in which these individuals engaged.

As far as translations of foreign economic literature are concerned, they were undertaken primarily by non-economists. Discussion of the types of foreign books which were translated into Dutch has been reserved for a later chapter. H. W. Tydeman (1778–1863), however, one of the earliest economics professors in Holland, was responsible for a number of translations. It is not entirely clear whether he was actually the translator of books or merely supervised the work of other translators. At any rate he provided prefaces and comments to five different translations and it is reasonable to assume that these works were translated primarily through Tydeman's initiative.[14] He was the only economics professor who devoted time to this aspect of economic literature.

Since there were no Dutch economic journals to be found at the start of the nineteenth century, articles on economic subjects had to be published in newspapers and periodicals of more general character. A number of economists in the nineteenth century undertook the founding of journals either dedicated to a particular problem area of economics or for the purpose of spreading economic knowledge in general. H. W. Tydeman was the earliest economist to found a journal, and he dedicated his journal to problems of poverty and to reviews of literature on this subject, *Magazijn voor het Armwezen* (Magazine for Pauperism). Tydeman published several articles in the journal and remained the leading editor during its lifespan, 1817–1822. Jan Ackersdijck founded a journal in 1844, *Bijdragen tot de Kennis der Nederlandsche en Vreemde Kolonieen* (Contributions to the knowledge of Dutch and foreign colonies). This journal was discontinued three years later because of lack of subscribers. Otto Van Rees originated a journal called *Pantheon* (subtitled: a journal for the spreading of useful knowledge), which was published from 1853–1858. This journal was founded primarily for the education of lower classes, to which Van Rees contributed not only by writing articles but also by giving evening lectures on subjects of economic nature.[15] Simon Vissering served as editor of *De Gids* for a period of forty-two years, and also wrote for several newspapers early in his career.[16] *De Gids* was a journal devoted to literature, culture, and science in general; it was founded in 1837, and included many papers and

---

[14] Translations by Tydeman: A. and P. W. Alison, *De Staatszorg voor de Armen Verdedigd en Aangeprezen* ("A Justification and Evaluation of Provision For the Poor by the State"), translated from the English (Leiden, 1853); Mrs. Marcet, *Grondbeginselen der Staats-Huishoudkunde in Gemeenzame Gesprekken* ("Conversations on Political Economy"), translated from the fourth English edition of 1821 (Dordrecht, 1825); Mrs. Marcet, *Jan Hopkens; Gewichtige Waarheden In Den Vorm Van Vertelselen* ("John Hopkins' notions on political economy"), translated from a French translation by Mad. De Cherbuliez (Utrecht, 1840); N. W. Senior, *Grondbeginselen der Staathuishoudkunde* (Principles of Political Economy"), from the lessons of Graaf Arrivabene in French, (Leiden, 1839); August Ludwig Von Schloezer, *Theorie Der Statistiek of* Staatkunde ("Theory of Statistics"), from the German edition in 1804 (Groningen, 1814). On Tydeman see: *N. N. B. W.*, II, 1461–1464, and J. W. Tydeman, "Levensbericht Van Mr. Hendrik Willem Tydeman," *Levensberichten van de Afgestorvene Leden der Maatschappij der Nederlandsche Letterkunde* (1863), pp. 403–450.

[15] About Van Rees see: *N. N. B. W.*, III, 1046–1047.

[16] About Vissering see: *N. N. B. W.*, X, 1119–1122.

book reviews in the field of economics, during its early period. C. A. Den Tex was one of the founders of a journal in 1825, called *Bijdragen tot regtsgeleerdheid en wetgeving*. Though this was predominantly a law journal "Contributions to the knowledge of law and legislation," reviews and papers on subjects of economics were frequently published in it. Jeronimo De Bosch Kemper was founder of the *Staatkundig en Staathuishoudkundig Jaarboekje* (Yearbook of Political Science and Economics), 1849–1884, to which he was an important contributor for many years. Besides *De Economist* it was one of the most important economic journals in Holland at the time.

Economists were also called upon for service on governmental committees and commissions organized for the investigation of certain economic questions and for the collection of statistics. Jan Ackersdijck was a member of a governmental committee for the regulation of higher education in 1828, and chairman of the National Commission for Statistics (Rijkscommissie voor Statistiek) from 1859 to 1860.[17] He was also a member of the "Union for Statistics," Vereeniging voor de Statistiek, founded by De Bosch Kemper in 1849, which was to compile and publish annual statistical material. Otto Van Rees was an active member of the Union for Statistics from 1858 to 1868. Simon Vissering was one of the original founders of the Union for Statistics, acted as chairman of the Union in 1876, was a member of the National Commission for Statistics from 1858 to 1861, and was chairman of the Commission during part of this time. In 1869 Vissering was chairman of the Statistical Congress held in The Hague.[18] It was primarily the initiative of Jeronimo De Bosch Kemper which brought about the founding of the Union for Statistics in 1849.[19] J. T. Buys served an important function as chairman of a different type of commission, namely, a commission for the regulation of the fisheries, from 1857 to 1893.[20]

[17] W. C. Mees, "Levensbericht van Mr. Jan Ackersdijck," *Levensberichten Der Afgestorvene Medeleden Van De Maatschappij Der Nederlandsche Letterkunde* (Leiden, 1862), pp. 25–47.

[18] On Vissering see *N. N. B. W.*, *ibid*; "Simon Vissering," in *Eigen Haard*, No. 41 (1879), pp. 411–414; and also H. B. Greven, "Simon Vissering," *Almanak Van Het Leidsche Studentencorps* 1889, pp. 359–367.

[19] C. A. Verrijn Stuart, *Inleiding Tot De Beoefening Der Statistiek*, I (Haarlem, 1910), 98.

[20] On Buys see: *N. N. B. W.*, X, 162–166.

The political functions which economists undertook or which were assigned to them are also notable. Three different types of governmental offices were held by economists: membership in the Second Chamber of the States General, representative in the Provincial States, and representative in the Municipal Council. A brief description of the nature of these offices is in order. After 1848 members of the Second Chamber were elected by citizens on the basis of proportional representation, for a period of four years. The Second Chamber consisted of 100 members. Between 1848 and 1917 members of the Second Chamber received a remuneration of 2,000 fl. Because there was no desire to encourage the development of professional politicians in Holland, compensation for political services was intentionally maintained at a low level. The two Chambers of the States General together with the King (or Queen) constitute the legislative power of the Dutch government. Members of the Provincial States, the legislative bodies of the provinces, are elected directly by residents of the provinces, for a period of four years. Again the election is based on proportional representation. The Municipal Council is a legislative as well as an executive organ. The size of the council varies with the population of the municipality. Members of the Municipal Council are also chosen directly by residents of the municipality.[21]

Jan Ackersdijck, although only for a short period, was a member of the Municipal Council of Utrecht and also a member of the Provincial State of Utrecht. Van Rees was a member of the Municipal Council of Utrecht from 1855 to 1858. In 1879 Simon Vissering resigned from his professorship at the University of Leiden to serve as Minister of Finance from 1879 to 1881. Den Tex was a member of the Second Chamber of the States General from 1842 to 1847 and a member of the Double Chamber in 1848.[22] De Bosch Kemper was a representative in the Municipal Council of Amsterdam and for some time served in the Provincial State of the province North-Holland as well. De Bosch Kemper was also a member of the Second Chamber for a short period. The above list of different types of functions sums up the variety of extra-curricular activities in which Dutch economics professors participated.

[21] Vandenbosch, Amry and Samuel J. Eldersveld, *Government of the Netherlands* (Lexington, 1947). See especially pp. 25–35, 73–79, 119–130.
[22] By Double Chamber is meant a joint session of First and Second Chamber.

Economists with Alternative Positions

Excluded from the discussion so far have been three figures whose careers in economics were not realized in an academic setting but who yet made important contributions to Dutch economics. W. C. Mees (1813–1884) was one of the most outstanding economists of nineteenth-century Holland. Mees was a devoted student of Ackersdijck, who was his uncle as well as his teacher. Mees had a very short teaching career; he taught one course in economics at a secondary school in Rotterdam, during a period when no one else could be found for the post. He also taught an economics course for adults during the year 1848 to 1849. While he had these two teaching experiences he was employed as secretary of the Chamber of Commerce of Rotterdam. During the last thirty-five years of his life Mees worked for the Netherlands Bank, the central bank of Holland, first as secretary from 1849 to 1863, then as president from 1863 to 1884. Studies concerning the monetary sector of the economy became Mees' special field, though he did not write exclusively on subjects related to money and currency issues. Mees contributed to four reports of governmental committees investigating the circulation of foreign currencies, two of which were published in 1855 and the others in 1872. Mees also served as the Dutch representative at international monetary conventions in Paris in 1867 and 1878. Though Mees may not have participated in as great a variety of activities as did some of his contemporaries, he was undoubtedly one of the most important Dutch economists of the period. This is clearly reflected by the calibre of his writings and in his banking career.[23]

J. L. De Bruyn Kops (1822–1887), though primarily a politician, made contributions to economics which ought not be neglected. Early in his life De Bruyn Kops accepted employment with the Department of Finance. From 1864 to 1868 he taught economics at the Poly technical School in Delft, an institution of secondary education primarily for engineers. In 1868 he was elected for membership in the Second Chamber of the States General. He maintained this political role for almost twenty years (1868–1887).

[23] About Mees see: *N. N. B. W.*, IV, 962–963; N. G. Pierson, "Levensbericht Van Mr. W. C. Mees," *Verspreide Economische Geschriften* van Pierson, II, 326–339; S. Vissering, "Levensbericht Van Mr. Willem Cornelis Mees," in *Verzamelde Geschriften* van Vissering (Leiden, 1889), I, 221–262; and "Twee Levensberichten," *De Economist*, XXXIV, Part I (1885), 210–215 (no author).

Credit should be given him primarily for having been a popularizer of economics at a time when the field was found in a state of relative neglect. In 1850 he wrote the first handbook of economics ever to appear in the Dutch language, *Beginselen van Staathuis-houdkunde*, a work that was revised four times. In 1852 De Bruyn Kops founded *De Economist*, which was the second Dutch periodical devoted to general economics, and which even today is one of the leading Dutch economic journals. De Bruyn Kops contributed innumerable articles to the journal, of which he remained editor throughout his life. He also wrote articles in several of the previously mentioned journals. He was one of the founders of the Union for Statistics in 1857, and was chairman of the Union from 1880 to 1883; he was also chairman of a governmental commission for the investiation of circulation of foreign currencies in Holland in 1860 and the Dutch degelate at the "Congrès Scientifique des Institutions de Prévoyance" in 1883. De Bruyn Kops' contributions are not marked by originality; however, his role in the diffusion of economics in Holland through his own writings and through his assistance in setting up organs of communication was decisive in stimulating academic economics.[24]

The last person to be included in this section is B. W. A. E. Sloet Tot Oldhuis (1808–1884), also a student of Jan Ackersdijck at the University of Utrecht. His career was comparable to that of De Bruyn Kops in that it was primarily political. Shortly after Sloet received his law degree he became Burgomaster (Head of the Municipal Council) of Hengelo, for a short period. In 1838 he became member and subsequently president of the court of justice of Zwolle and also a representative in the Provincial State of the province of Overijsel. From 1848 to 1860 Sloet was a member of the Second Chamber, while he also belonged to the Double Chamber in 1840 and in 1848. His contribution to economics was primarily his founding and editorship of the first Dutch general economics journal *Tijdschrift voor Staathuishoud-kunde en Statistiek* (Journal for economics and statistics) which

---

[24] About De Bruyn Kops see: *N. N. B. W.*, III, 715–716; "Mr. J. L. De Bruyn Kops" in *Eigen Haard* (1887), pp. 532–536 (no author); Mr. J. K. W. Quarles Van Ufford, "Levensbericht van Mr. Jacob Leonard De Bruyn Kops," *Levensberichten Der Afgestorven Medeleden Van De Maatschappij Der Nederlandsche Letterkunde* (1889), pp. 29–56; J. K. W. Quarles Van Ufford, "In Memoriam," *De Economist*, XXXVI (1887), Part II, 862–867; P. Hennipman, "J. L. De Bruyn Kops," *De Economist*, C (1952), 785–815.

appeared from 1841 to 1875. Contrary to the title of the Journal it offered little in the way of statistics. Sloet wrote a considerable number of articles in it, reviewed foreign and Dutch economic literature, and discussed most dissertations on topics of interest to students of economics. In his journal Sloet also presented translations of parts of Harriet Martineau's *Illustrations of Political Economy*, and sections of a work on colonies by Wilhelm Roscher. Furthermore, Sloet provided a Dutch translation of *Elements d'économie politique* by Joseph Droz, in 1849, which was sufficiently popular in Holland to call for a second edition in 1850. Finally, Sloet translated a handbook of economics written by the Frenchman Etienne Dumont, *Handboekje der Staathuishoudkunde*, which allegedly was based on the writings of Jeremy Bentham. This work was Sloet's last translation and was published in 1851. It is primarily on the basis of his literary efforts in the field of economics that Sloet Tot Oldhuys should be included in a list of contributors to the nineteenth-century developments of Dutch economics.[25]

The most important professional features in the lives of representative economists have been mentioned, with the object of focusing on different aspects of the relationship between human agents and the economic discipline. The backgrounds of these individual economists cannot be dissociated from their attitudes toward economic problems and from their outlook upon economics as a discipline. Though inferences must be reserved until the economic ideas of these men have been presented, some generalizations can be made here about the career patterns of Dutch economists in the nineteenth century.

Some Generalizations about the Careers of Dutch Economists

In the course of the nineteenth century economists assumed an ever more important role in Holland, and their lives were characterized by participation in diversified functions. Within the academic sphere little change can be noticed with regard to the status of the economist. But outside of the university the economist was gradually called upon to carry out a variety of alternative duties, as is demonstrated by the career patterns of above economists.

[25] About Sloet Tot Oldhuis see: *N. N. B. W.*, II, 1325–1326; "Twee Levensberichten," in *De Economist*, XXXIV (1885), Part I, 205–210.

Though Adriaan Kluit and H. W. Tydeman at the start of the century were involved solely in teaching, this was not true of any subsequent economist.

An increasing interest of the state in the compilation of data on various aspects of the Dutch economy, led to the organization of governmental commissions for investigatory and at times for regulatory purposes. A number of economists, on grounds of their special qualifications, were called upon to serve on commissions such as those concerned with educational problems, currency problems, with the railroad system and with the fisheries. Not all of these services represented long term commitments of economists, but in several cases economists were connected with these commissions for a number of years.

It also becomes evident that most economists after Ackersdijck were engaged in the institutionalization of statistics in Holland. Either as members of or in executive capacities in the National Commission for Statistics (founded in 1858) or in the Union for Statistics (founded in 1849) economists worked on the standardization of statistical compilations and the development of statistical techniques. These economists actively contributed to the collection of statistics as is revealed in their many articles in statistical journals and their cooperative efforts at statistical publications.

Most striking perhaps in the survey of life histories is the number of political offices held by Dutch economists during some part of their lives. Two members of the group. De Bruyn Kops and Sloet Tot Oldhuis, devoted the major part of their lives to political careers. But also, most of the professors have somewhere along the line held political offices at one level of government or another. In some cases the political office was held simultaneously with a university chair, and not infrequently the political function developed rather late in the life of the economist. It thus appears that at least outside of the university system the economist was gaining recognition. Although the variety of positions open to nineteenth-century economists is not impressive when compared to present-day opportunities, the impression is conveyed that economists in Holland were undergoing professionalization during the period under consideration. Thus it is possible to look upon the founding of journals as an aspect of professionalization, in the sense that economists gradually became aware that they constituted a group concerned with a unique area of investigation and problems, requiring its own periodical literature as a means of communication. An increasing number of positions developed in central banking, chambers of commerce and in various governmental organs, which were to be filled specifically by economists.

Professionalization of economists in the non-academic world preceded recognition of economics as an autonomous field of investigation in the educational system. The development of economics as a separate university faculty has been discussed in the previous chapter. It will be recalled that the establishment of the Rotterdam School of Economics in 1913, which symbolized the emancipation of economics from the law faculty, was sponsored primarily by commercial interest groups. The minimal role of academic economists in this development indicates the lack of identification of the professor of economics with the discipline of economics, as a domain peculiarly his own. Within the realm of the university, the economics professor could only identify himself with lawyers, who were his colleagues in the law faculty at which he occupied a chair. The idea that he was an economist, possibly qualified for a specialized career which was professionally distinguishable from a law career, did not suggest itself to the academic economist in the context of his status in the university structure.

CONTRIBUTORS WHO WERE NOT ECONOMISTS

Since all Dutch economics professors were required to teach statistics as well as economics at the law faculties of universities, and since most nineteenth-century economists were in some way involved with the development of statistics, an intimate tie between economics and statistics was maintained throughout the century. In connection with the linkage of economics and statistics in Holland two additional figures, who were not economists, will be introduced here because of the significant role they played in the development of statistics.

The advancement of Dutch statistics during the nineteenth century was encouraged at first not from the point of view of de-

veloping a tool for scientific disciplines, but for the purpose of ful-
filling certain needs of the state. As the role of the state with
respect to social and economic affairs expanded in Holland at the
start of the nineteenth century, an increasing need for statistical
data manifested itself in connection with planning and policy
formation. Napoleon has been held responsible for instilling the
Dutch with an interest in statistics early in the nineteenth century, when Holland was annexed temporarily by the French empire.[26]
It was Napoleon who introduced registers of marriages, births, and
deaths for all communities in Holland and thus initiated the
compilation of organized vital statistics.

A mathematician of Portuguese descent, Rehuel Lobatto (1797–
1866), an official in the Department of Internal Affairs of the
Dutch government, was primarily engaged in the compilation and
organization of official statistics. Lobatto had been a student of
Quetelet in Brussels, and jointly with Quetelet he edited *Correspondance Mathématique et Physique.* Early in the nineteenth
century it became practice in Holland to gather statistics on
imports, exports, goods in transit, education and pauper relief.
The availability of statistical material of this type induced
Lobatto to publish a statistical yearbook, which appeared continuously from 1826 to 1849. In 1831 Lobatto became secretary of
a statistical commission for the study and editing of assembled
statistical material. In 1841 Lobatto was appointed by Minister of
Finance Rochussen to serve as member of a commission for the
conversion of the public debt, and in 1842 he became teacher of
higher mathematics at the Polytechnical School in Delft. Lobatto
deserves mention here because of his efforts toward standardizing
statistical methods, in the tradition of Quetelet, and also because
he published the first Dutch statistical annual for a period of
twenty-three years.[27]

Marie Matthieu Von Baumhauer (1816–1878) who had been a
lawyer originally, continued the work of Lobatto. In 1848 Von
Baumhauer became director of a newly established statistical
bureau in the Department of Internal Affairs. In 1851 the new

[26] C. A. Verrijn Stuart, "The History and Development of Statistics in the
Netherlands," in *The History of Statistics* by John Koren (New York, 1918), pp. 427–445.
[27] About Lobatto see: *N, N, B, W.,* VI, 958; *The Jewish Encyclopedia,* VIII, 146;
and C. A. Verrijn Stuart, "The History and Development of Statistics in the Netherlands," *op. cit.,* pp. 432–433.

bureau began to publish a statistical annual (Statistisch Jaarboek) which was an expanded version of Lobatto's yearbook. The censuses of 1849, 1859, and 1869 were conducted under the direction of Von Baumhauer. He was also the first to compile mortality tables from census data of the Netherlands. The statistical yearbook was published by Von Baumhauer's bureau from 1851 to 1868. Von Baumhauer remained director of the commission from 1848 to 1876. He was also the Dutch representative at International Statistical Congresses in the years 1853 to 1875.[28]

Lobatto and Von Baumhauer were the only non-economists of significance in the setting up of organizations for the collection of statistics and the standardization of statistical methods. Another group of non-economists, who in some sense can be looked upon as contributors to the development of economics in Holland in the nineteenth century, were the translators of foreign economic literature. As noted previously, there were only two economists who had concerned themselves with translations. Most of the foreign economic works were translated into Dutch by non-economists. In several of the translated works there is no preface or name of the translator to be found, so that one cannot trace the initiative or responsibility for the translations. In other cases the title of the translator indicates that he was a lawyer or a schoolteacher in the elementary or secondary school system. Some of the Dutch versions of foreign economics books include prefaces but usually the translator fails to explain why he chose to translate a particular book. Because of lacking information the persons responsible for translations become irrelevant and the translated works must be considered on the basis of their own merit and influence. The types of economics books which were translated into the Dutch language during the nineteenth century will be considered in Chapter VII.

In this chapter the career patterns of representative Dutch economists have been dealt with. The professional life of economists with academic careers, as well as of those who pursued careers outside the academic world have been examined. The various roles engaged in by nineteenth-century Dutch economists, in universities as well as in the world of politics have also been

---

[28] About Von Baumhauer see: *N. N. B. W.*, X, 34; C. A. Verrijn Stuart, *ibid.*, pp. 433–436.

reviewed. Furthermore, two men who were not economists by profession have been included in the discussion, because they contributed to the developments of economics and/or statistics. A chart has been added to facilitate comparison of professional-biographical data on representative Dutch nineteenth-century economists. It was felt that the above information would shed light on the professional status of economics in Holland during the nineteenth century.

CHAPTER VI

DUTCH ECONOMIC THOUGHT 1800–1870: ITS NATURE

In this chapter we are concerned with the nature of Dutch economic thought as depicted in the major writings of representative Dutch economists of the period under consideration. It is assumed that these major writings reflect what was typical of Dutch economic thought in most of the nineteenth century despite the fact that ideas of people other than economists are not considered.

It is hoped that an account of representative economic literature of the period will shed light on the following aspects of economic thinking: (1) the distribution of interest among various topics and among the different fields of economics; (2) the distribution of concern between theoretical and applied economics; (3) the continuity and (4) the degree of originality in Dutch economic thought. At the close of the chapter we shall return to these considerations.

The writings of Dutch economists fall roughly into three categories: (1) policy-oriented, (2) historical, and (3) abstract-theoretical. There is of course some overlap between any two of these categories. Historical investigations may have been prompted by questions of economic policy much as policy oriented writings sometimes were based upon theoretical formulations. However, the distinction between the three classes of writings does serve a purpose, particularly in regard to point (2) above. It will be found that the first category includes the bulk of major writings by Dutch economists.

The chapter will be organized around the main topics to which Dutch economists addressed themselves. Policy-oriented writings will be examined in Part I, Historical writings in Part II, and

Theoretical writings in Part III. Part IV will be devoted to some generalizations concerning the nature of Dutch economic thought.

POLICY-ORIENTED WRITINGS

Dutch economic literature devoted to questions of economic policy can be grouped around the following topics: (1) Pauperism, Population, and Wages; (2) the Corn Laws; (3) Currency problems; (4) Banking issues; and (5) Public Finance. The discussion will proceed in the above order.

Pauperism, Population, and Wages

Especially around the middle of the nineteenth century questions relating to pauperism constituted one of the most talked about issues. Pauperism was usually discussed in the context of population growth, and to the extent that economists at that time gave thought to wages, this subject also was related to pauperism and population growth. The writers under consideration were primarily concerned with the following questions: had pauperism increased or diminished since the previous century? What were the main causes of pauperism? What type of remedial action could be suggested?

The inclusion of some factual information on poverty in Holland is called for. Though demographic statistics are available for nineteenth-century Holland, figures on unemployment and wage levels appear to be non-existent. With the exception of a few years the population of Holland expanded continuously though unevenly during the period of 1815 to 1879.[1] Population growth during the period 1800 to 1910 has been estimated at an average annual rate of 9.2 per 1000.[2] Decennial population figures for Holland have been presented in Chapter II. It has also been said of the early nineteenth-century Dutch population that it consisted of rich and poor people while lacking a middle class, that unemployment brought about emigration, and that a "back to rural areas"

---

[1] J. C. G. Evers, *Bijdrage tot de Bevolkingsleer van Nederland*, p. 9. The population decreased during 1847–1848, 1849–1850, and 1869–1870.

[2] Ludwig Elster, "Der Bevölkerungsstand und die Bevölkerungsbewegung der neuesten Zeit bis zum Ausbruch des Weltkrieges," *Handwörterbuch Der Staatswissenschaften*, Vierte Auflage, II (Jena, 1924), 688–689.

movement was taking place with the result that the number of inhabitants of many cities was diminishing.[3]

As far as unemployment is concerned the following information may be cited. At the beginning of the nineteenth century work-houses were set up for the unemployed in many Dutch cities, by churches and private charity organizations. These institutions primarily sponsored spinning, weaving, and knitting, but most of them failed to meet the competition of existing textile industries.[4] In 1818 a law was passed which made each municipality responsible for its needy, provided that an individual's residence in the municipality, for at least four years, could be established. As of 1818 a welfare organization (Maatschappij van Weldadigheid) founded agricultural settlement colonies with the objective of creating employment opportunities. After 1825 this project received financial assistance from the government. The number of beggars drafted for these colonies increased from 1,053 in 1823 to 5,490 in 1848.[5]

Distress reached its maximum during the 1840's, and around 1848 legislative regulation of pauperism was proposed. In 1854 a law was passed which again left major responsibility for the poor with churches and private institutions for charity, though it included provisions for public relief when absolutely necessary.[6] The evidence presented indicates that problems of unemployment and urban poverty were widespread in the Dutch economy during the early nineteenth century.

There was considerable disagreement among Dutch economists about the state of pauperism in Holland around the 1850's. One group of economists pointed toward a supposed increase in pauperism, supporting their position with statistics on charity, public relief and the growth of institutions for the destitute. Another group questioned the reality of increasing poverty and refused to accept the inference that statistics indicating increases in relief were indicative of increasing poverty. The latter group argued that the mere fact that a society at a given time makes larger pro-

---

[3] Leonie Van Nierop, *De Bevolkingsbeweging der Nederlandsche Stad* (Amsterdam, 1905), pp. 93–94, 98, 108.

[4] Ph. Falkenburg, "Armengesetzgebung in den Niederlanden," *Handwörterbuch Der Staatswissenschaften*, Dritte Auflage, II (Jena, 1909), 113–119.

[5] Falkenburg, *op. cit.*, pp. 114–115; Van Nierop, *op. cit.*, p. 107.

[6] Falkenburg, *op. cit.*, p. 115; Baasch, *op. cit.*, p. 536.

visions for the needy than it had done previously, was no evidence
of a trend of growing poverty. Although adequacy of the statistics
then available was quite open to dispute, economists of the second
group were unable to verify their position, i.e., that pauperism
had not increased in Holland.

The first author to infer an increase in destitution from the
available statistics on relief and philanthropical aid was G. Luttenberg.[7] Subsequently similar statistics were made use of in a
series of studies on pauperism.[8] Vissering and De Bosch Kemper
on the other hand contended that inferences about poverty from
statistics on charity tended to be invalid for the following reasons:
changes had taken place in methods of compilation; the statistics
referred to included persons who had been supported for only a
few weeks of a year as well as persons who received income supplements though they were fully employed; an individual would appear in the statistics several times if he was subsidized by more
than one institution. The two writers were therefore of the opinion
that statistics on charity and relief were not suited or designed to
provide an accurate index of pauperism.

The position of representative economists, on the state of
pauperism, may be summarized about as follows: H.W.Tydeman,
together with J. Heemskerk and J. W. Tydeman, found evidence
for the increasing severity of the problem of destitution in Holland.
W. C. Mees and J. L. De Bruyn Kops, though uncertain whether
they succeeded in verifying an increase in pauperism, were concerned about the gravity of the situation and urged for economic
analysis of the problem. De Bosch Kemper and Vissering were
inclined to believe that pauperism was no more of a problem than
it had been during preceding centuries, that a certain amount of
poverty was inevitable and due to faults of the poor themselves,
and that most likely the needy had become less poor, in an absolute
sense even if the contrast between rich and poor had widened.[9]

---

[7] G. Luttenberg, *Proeve van Onderzoek omtrent het Armwezen in ons Vaderland*
(Amsterdam, 1841).

[8] See Simon Vissering, "Regeling Van Het Armwezen," 1852 in *Herinneringen*, II,
190–196, where he reviewed these studies.

[9] H. W. Tydeman, J. Heemskerk, and J. W. Tydeman, *Denkbeelden Omtrent Eene
Wettelijke Regeling Van Het Armwezen in Nederland* (Amsterdam, 1850). W. C. Mees,
De Werkinrigtingen Voor Armen Uit Een Staathuishoudkundig Oogpunt Beschouwd
(Rotterdam, 1844); S. Vissering, "Regeling Van Het Armwezen," *op. cit.*, J. L.
De Bruyn Kops, *Korte Beschouwingen Over Het Armwezen* (Leyden en Amsterdam,

Viewpoints regarding the causes of pauperism will further clarify the ideas of these economists.

Those writers who denied that distress had become increasingly severe during the first part of the nineteenth century were less preoccupied with the causes of pauperism than were their opponents. De Bosch Kemper found the main causes of poverty to be lack of skill, lack of productive effort, wastefulness, and above all, heavy drinking. He did not find that Holland was overpopulated; nor did he find that the number of workers exceeded employment opportunities. But he admitted that there were too many unskilled and too few skilled workers, a fact which he attributed to the frequency of marriage at a premature age. De Bosch Kemper also rejected shortage of capital and raw materials, or the incidence of heavy taxes on necessities, as causes, of poverty. The reasons for poverty were associated by him with the poor themselves rather than with the economic system.[10]

Vissering divided the causes of poverty into two categories: (1) the natural or inevitable causes, outside the realm of human intervention, such as accidents, diseases, theft, and death of the provider of a family; and (2) self-imposed causes which were due to the weaknesses of individuals such as lack of training, laziness, wastefulness, irresponsibility, etc. Vissering, as did De Bosch Kemper, put primary emphasis on the poor themselves as being responsible for their poverty; he considered the so-called natural or inevitable causes of poverty to be only of temporary and locally restricted incidence.[11]

De Bruyn Kops associated pauperism with the discontinuous character of production. He also admitted that the Dutch economy during the first part of the nineteenth century had not offered employment opportunities for the entire population. He remarked that population growth was disproportionate to capital formation in Holland, but he presented no data in support of this statement. It is evident, however, that in De Bruyn Kops' opinion the problem of pauperism rested basically on inadequacy of savings and a resulting lack of capital, factors which he considered responsible for limited employment opportunities. Both De Bruyn Kops and Mees

1851); J. De Bosch Kemper, *Geschiedkundig Onderzoek Naar De Armoede in Ons Vaderland* (Haarlem, 1851).

[10] De Bosch Kemper, *op. cit.*, pp. 190–192, 154–165, 168, 174, 251.

[11] Simon Vissering, *Handboek Van Praktische Staathuishoudkunde*, I, 353–358.

attributed the increase in pauperism largely to early marriages and a high birth rate, which presumably was characteristic of the lower classes in Holland at that time. Mees more than any other economist stressed overpopulation as the primary cause of unemployment and pauperism.[12]

In a review article on McCulloch's *Essay on the Circumstances which Determine the Rate of Wages*, J. T. Buys inserted comments which have some bearing on the question of poverty in Holland. Buys tried to account for the relatively small amount of improvement in the living standard of the Dutch working class, when compared with that experienced by the rest of the population. He attributed this condition in part to the high prices of foods, which compared unfavorably with the prices of manufactured goods. He pointed out that since heavy taxes on necessities had kept food prices extremely high in Holland, and since the worker spent most of his income on foods, the latter was experiencing a growing discrepancy between his money income and his cost of living. Buys therefore considered the tax structure partly responsible for destitution but he also found that the practices of charitable institutions had diffused the impact of poverty, for he claimed that relief organizations, by granting wage supplements to the destitute, had inadvertently supported low wage levels. These organizations were thus counteracting the material advancement of workers by enabling a part of the labor force to work for less than subsistence wages.[13] The approach of Buys, Mees, and De Bruyn Kops in analyzing pauperism is thus comparable, in that each of these writers looked for extra-individual variables, i.e., lack of educational opportunities, lack of employment possibilities, and the tax structure as factors responsible for poverty.

Economists also disputed respecting the poverty-alleviating capacity of the state. Thus, Tydeman, Heemskerk, and Tydeman came to the conclusion that poverty should not be regarded as an abnormal condition, that it would always exist in some form, and that therefore the government must take legislative action and prescribe and delimit the conditions of relief.[14] De Bruyn Kops and Mees, on the contrary, were in favor of state intervention as

---

[12] De Bruyn Kops, *op. cit.*, pp. 15–18, 36, 41–43; Mees, *op. cit.*, p. 30.
[13] J. T. Buys, "Over Arbeidsloonen," *De Economist*, II (1853), 371–384.
[14] Tydeman, Heemskerk, and Tydeman, *op. cit.*

long as it was of temporary nature only. In the long run, they felt, organized relief provided by the state would lead to economic mis-allocations. Vissering went further and urged that the government not intervene on behalf of those who were unable to provide their subsistence.

W. C. Mees was primarily interested in determining whether and to what extent workhouses for the poor could be expected to offer a solution to the problem of destitution. The diminution of poverty in a society, according to Mees, depended in the long run on moral and intellectual advancement of the people. Progress along these lines, stated Mees, would lead to later marriages, to postponement of procreation until people were able to support their young, as well as to greater competence, trustworthiness, and parsimony. Mees attributed destitution to overpopulation of the working class. Under some circumstances, stated Mees, work-houses could aggravate the population problem. Public works could also be hazardous for the economy at large, since they might channel capital and market demand away from private enterprise, which, according to Mees, was always more efficient than public enterprise. Mees recommended workhouses only when they were geared to train youth and develop skills in the younger element of the population. Mees admitted that workhouses might supply temporary relief of unemployment, but he considered their aggre-gate effect, when viewed in the context of the entire economy, to be more harmful than remedial.[15]

In the opinion of De Bruyn Kops the ultimate alleviation of poverty rested on stabilization in the level of production, the removal of constricting influences which interfered with pro-duction, and the moral and intellectual development of mankind. De Bruyn Kops was as convinced as Mees that in the long run the problem of destitution had to be solved in the realm of education. Expansion of educational opportunities would raise the productive capacities of the poor through acquisition of skills, knowledge about health and nutrition, and awareness of the importance of parsimony. Education and enlightenment, stated De Bruyn Kops, should prevent any future imbalance between population and capital formation.[16]

[15] W. C. Mees, *op. cit.*, pp. 36, 51, 84, 118, 243.
[16] J. L. De Bruyn Kops, *Beginselen Van Staathuishoudkunde*, pp. 507–509.

In the immediate, however, said De Bruyn Kops, the destitution problem required governmental aid until a balance between number of workers and employment possibilities had been restored. He was much concerned about the growing number of beggars, which he felt had a demoralizing effect on society. The prevention of begging, according to De Bruyn Kops, was to be considered as much a responsibility of the government as was the provision of public safety. It was on these grounds that he favored governmental assistance to the destitute in the form of public works, relief, or a combination of both. De Bruyn Kops was thus an advocate of governmental intervention during a transitional period only, and he explicitly disclaimed being a proponent of "le droit du travail," a principle quite widely endorsed in Western Europe in the mid-nineteenth century.[17]

As mentioned previously, Vissering opposed all forms of governmental aid to the poor. To this economist there appeared to be an inevitable relation between governmental relief of poverty and an increase in the number of poor. Vissering did not want the responsibility for earning a living to be transferred from the individual to society. He claimed to be in agreement with Malthus on this point. His attitude towards governmental responsibility for relief of pauperism was thus in complete agreement, he believed, with that of J. R. McCulloch. Vissering cited McCulloch's *Principles of Political Economy*, to the effect that state intervention had been rejected on principle and in practice. Vissering even contended that governmental support of the unemployed was likely to prepare the road to communism.[18]

[17] De Bruyn Kops, *Korte Beschouwingen Over Het Armwezen*, pp. 40, 44, 48. De Bruyn Kops maintained his position on the question of poverty despite charges that he was advocating communism. A. Elink Sterk, Jr., *Eenige Bedenkingen op het Geschrift van Mr. J. L. De Bruyn Kops over het Beginsel van Armenverzorging door den Staat* ('S Gravenhage, 1852); S. Vissering, "Regeling Van Het Armwezen," *op. cit.*, pp. 290–291.

[18] S. Vissering, "Regeling Van Het Armwezen," *op. cit.*, pp. 227–229, 244. Though Vissering showed little concern for living conditions of the poor in his discussion of pauperism, it may be noted here that he discussed the exceptionally low nutritional standard in Holland in another article, "Over Werkloonen en Volksvoeding," in *Herinneringen*, II, 268–292. In this article he admitted that the Dutch were about as undernourished as the Irish, since the potato represented the main component of the Dutch diet. Vissering stated that because of high excise taxes on foods, the worker could only afford potatoes. Vissering also blamed Dutch tax policy for the lowness of wages in Holland, an argued for a change in the tax structure. In this context vissering showed a less affirmative regard for the standard of living of Dutch workers

In summary, it may be said that there were two schools of thought on the question of pauperism in Holland around the middle of the nineteenth century. One group of economists showed great concern for the extent of unemployment and poverty, attributed it primarily to overpopulation and maladjustments in the economy, and recommended state intervention at least for a transitional period. This group included Tydeman, Mees, and De Bruyn Kops. Another group of economists, including De Bosch Kemper and Vissering, saw no need for new methods of coping with poverty, mainly blamed the lower classes for their poor living conditions since it was up to the individual to improve himself, and opposed even temporary assistance by the government.

Corn Laws

Dutch economic thought during the period under consideration may be characterized in broad terms as a quest for liberalism. Although there were differences in the views and emphases of leading Dutch economists, they pleaded unanimously for laissez faire in most spheres of economic activity. The particular orientation of individual economists in regard to commercial freedom will be discussed in the next chapter where foreign influences on economic thinkers will be traced. It is sufficient to mention here that, in the controversy between protectionistic and free-trade groups during the early part of the century, economists always supported the free trade position.

Insofar as early nineteenth-century Dutch economic policy is concerned, the years 1830–1850 represent a period of germination of free trade policy. The transition from mercantilistic economic policy under the reign of Willem I (1813–1840) to the free trade policy established during the second part of the century, was modeled after the liberalization taking place in England.[19] Orientation towards Britain manifested itself in economic-policy measures as well as in the attitudes of economists. In 1847, for example, two Dutch economists published a "History of Tariff Reforms in

than he had in his discussion of pauperism. For similar views on food taxes in Holland see J. T. Buys in *De Economist* (1853).

[19] F. J. De Jong, "Phoenix Vrijhandel: Van Het Naieve Naar Het Critische Vrijhandelspunt," *De Economist*, C (1952), 937; Z. W. Sneller, *Geschiedenis Van De Nederlandsche Landbouw, 1795–1940*, p. 49.

England," for the purpose of stimulating the introduction of similar policies in Holland.[20]

During the first part of the nineteenth century Dutch economic policy often conflicted with the views of leading economists. However, since liberalism manifested itself increasingly in policy formation during the second half of the century. Dutch economists were less frequently compelled to write about issues of trade policy after than before 1850. A discussion of the corn laws by two prominent economists exemplifies how Dutch economists viewed problems of commercial policy and illustrates the tendency of the Dutch to follow the British in respect to trade-policy reforms.

For over two centuries Dutch merchants had dominated the European grain trade with the result that Holland was often referred to as the regulating granary. Various seventeenth-century writers as Dirk Graswinckel, Pieter de la Court, and his brother Jan de la Court, had insisted on freedom for the grain trade.[21] As Ackersdijck remarked: "the principle of free grain trade was so to speak at home in Holland."[22]

A series of wars during the late eighteenth and early nineteenth centuries was followed by a period of rising grain prices which reached a peak in 1817. From then on grain prices tended downward, and this trend was accelerated by the appearance of a new and cheap source of supply, namely Russia.[23] High import duties and prohibitions deprived Holland after 1818 of her previous market outlets in England, France, Spain, and Portugal. In 1822 the Dutch adopted mildly restrictive import duties. But, after agitation for protective corn laws had made considerable headway, a high protective tariff was introduced in 1825. Along with the break-down of the Dutch-Belgian Union in 1830 came a reduction in import duties on grain back to the 1822 level. When prices declined again after 1830, a renewed demand for agricultural protection made itself heard. This eventually led to the introduction of a sliding scale of protective import duties in 1835, i.e., duties which rose and fell automatically along with price movements in the domestic grain market. This system of import

---

[20] D. A. Portielje and S. Vissering, *Geschiedenis Der Tariefhervorming in Engeland* (Amsterdam, 1847).

[21] Laspeyres, *op. cit.*, pp. 205–208.

[22] Jan Ackersdijck, *Bedenkingen over de Korenwetten* (Utrecht, 1835), p. 1.

[23] Baasch, *op. cit.*, p. 487.

duties was apparently copied from the British.[24] Moreover, the termination of corn laws practically coincided in England (1846) and Holland (1847), after both countries had suffered poor crops and potato blight. Low import duties on grain were thereafter maintained in Holland until 1877.[25]

The context just described is that in which Ackersdijck and Vissering formulated and expressed their ideas respecting the corn laws. Ackersdijck warned against the passing of a new corn law in 1835, the same year during which a sliding scale of import duties was instituted in Holland. He illustrated his misgivings about these corn laws with references to the British situation. Ackersdijck found it strange that the Dutch wanted to introduce a system which in England had led to serious criticism and bitter complaints. Presumably the purpose of the corn laws was to support the price of grain in order to protect agriculture. Yet nowhere, stated Ackersdijck, was agriculture in a more distressed condition than in England. What was nominally referred to as a measure in support of the farmer merely served to increase the incomes of landowners. Ackersdijck utilized Ricardian rent theory to trace through the process by which corn laws benefited the landlords.[26]

It was Ackersdijck's conviction that corn laws were burdensome to the entire economy for the following reasons: (1) the consequently higher grain prices put a greater burden on the poor than it did on the rich, since the tax was shared not in proportion to income but in proportion to the consumption of grain; (2) as a result of higher grain prices, the Dutch would be induced to produce grain on poor soil, and thus misallocate resources whereas it would be more economical to import grain; (3) rising food prices would put pressure on wages, and thus burden industry and give rise to poverty insofar as wages lagged behind prices; (4) a decrease in imports would inevitably bring about a reduction in exports. In Ackersdijck's opinion, theory and practice had shed much light on the disadvantages of corn laws, and he intended his pamphlet to make these drawbacks plain to the public.[27]

[24] Sneller, *op. cit.*, p. 49.
[25] Regarding the Dutch corn laws see: Sneller, *op. cit.*, pp. 48–50; I. J. Brugmans, "De Economische Conjunctuur in Nederland in de 19e Eeuw," *op. cit.*, pp. 108–111; Baasch, *op. cit.*, pp. 487–490.
[26] Ackersdijck, *op. cit.*, pp. 3, 7, 18, 30.
[27] Ackersdijck, *op. cit.*, pp. 20–28.

Simon Vissering published his ideas on the corn laws in a series of articles in a daily Amsterdam newspaper in 1845. In these articles Vissering pleaded for freedom of the grain trade, because it was to be considered as "the source and root of all Dutch commerce," and because the experience of the past had demonstrated a policy of non-interference most conducive to thriving commerce. Vissering pointed out that in Hamburg and Switzerland commerce had been flourishing during the past twenty-five years and that this prosperous situation was attributable entirely to the liberalization of trade restrictions. Vissering's arguments against the corn laws correspond largely to those of Ackersdijck. He claimed that all protection led to an imbalance of supply and demand as well as to an imbalance between the different fields of production. Furthermore, corn laws create a monopoly for landlords while leaving the farmer in poverty. This had been clearly demonstrated by the British experience.[28]

The discussion of the corn law problem by Ackersdijck and Vissering illustrates the general approach of Dutch economists to questions of trade policy. The objection of economists to non-agricultural protection was based on contentions very similar to those raised against the corn laws. On the subject of commercial policy Dutch economists argued invariably in favor of non-intervention. The position taken was usually supported with references to Dutch commercial policy during previous centuries, to views of antecedent Dutch economic thinkers, to conclusions derived from economic theory, to the experiences of other nations (especially England), and, to the extent that they were available, empirical data.

Currency Problems

During the time of the Dutch Republic and until 1816 the Dutch had adhered to a silver currency standard. The monetary act of 1816 established a bimetallic currency standard in Holland and determined the mint value of gold to be 15.87 times that of silver. The subsequent period from 1816 to 1845 was one of extreme disorder in the Dutch currency system. A part of the metallic curren-

---

[28] Simon Vissering, "De Vrije Graanhandel," a series of articles published during March and April in the *Algemeene Handelsblad* of 1845, reprinted in vol. II of *Herinneringen*, pp. 1–64, see especially pp. 3–5, 40–42, 60–62.

cy had a lower silver content than that which had been lawfully established, but the government postponed its plans for recoinage several times. Furthermore, there was a discrepancy between the mint and the market ratios of gold to silver, and gold was overvalued at the mint. In addition, the exchange rate between the French franc and the Dutch guilder was inappropriately determined and the guilder was undervalued relative to the franc. In Holland, therefore, though the country was nominally on a bimetallic standard, its undervalued money, i.e., silver, was driven out of circulation, and the Dutch monetary medium came to consist primarily of gold and of some debased silver coins.

A number of attempts were made to remedy the currency system initiated in 1816. In 1825 the French-Dutch exchange rate was adjusted. In 1839 the lawful silver weight of the guilder was reduced and adjusted to the silver-gold ratio. In 1845 a plan was put into effect through which the old silver coins were eventually to be withdrawn from circulation and replaced by new money. The year 1847 marks Holland's departure from a bimetallic currency. A silver standard was introduced, and this proved to be a satisfactory currency standard for Holland until the 1870's when silver currency was abandoned in most European countries. The views to be presented in this section grew out of discussions of the monetary problems current at the time.[29]

The writings of Jan Ackersdijck and W. C. Mees on the currency situation will be considered. Ackersdijck, in a pamphlet on "The Currency System of Holland," written in 1845, expressed serious concern about the inadequate regulation of Holland's circulating medium. He was especially provoked by the fact that the government had postponed recoinage time and again, allegedly because of the cost burden, even though a desparate need for recoinage had been obvious since the beginning of the century. In the same year that Ackersdijck's pamphlet appeared, a plan for recoinage was designed and put into effect soon thereafter. It was Ackersdijck's claim that the government's disregard for established economic principles was responsible for the delay in currency

---

[29] On the history of the Dutch nineteenth-century currency system see G. M. Verrijn Stuart, "Nieuwe Regeling Van Het Nederlandsche Muntwezen," *De Economist* XCV (1947), 309–360, especially 317–324; and N. G. Pierson, *Leerboek Der Staathuishoudkunde*, I (Haarlem, 1896), second edition, 473–483.

revision and for considerable monetary losses. Ackersdijck did not, however, specify the economic principles which the government should have pursued.[30]

Ackersdijck also pointed out that legislators should have foreseen the unfortunate consequences of the monetary act of 1816. In view of the inadequate franc-guilder exchange rate and the overvaluation of gold it was inevitable that silver would be driven out of circulation. Though he made no explicit reference to Gresham's law, he must have had this law in mind. Despite several warnings to the government, continued Ackersdijck, new silver coins were supplied even though it was known that they promptly would leave the country. From 1825 on the government pursued a policy of coining gold primarily, with the result that the bimetallic standard adopted in 1816 became in effect a gold standard. It was Ackersdijck's opinion that Holland should then have established the gold standard officially. Since he had doubts about the feasibility of a bimetallic standard, because of the need for constant adjustment of the relative mint values to changes in the relative market values of the two metals, he adopted the viewpoint of monometallism. Ackersdijck therefore opposed the monetary act of 1839, under which the gold-silver ratio was altered so that a double standard could be maintained in Holland.[31]

The remainder of Ackersdijck's pamphlet contained his criticism of the recoinage plan designed in 1845. This enabled Ackersdijck to express his distrust of paper money, since the government intended to substitute paper money temporarily for the metallic currency in order to withdraw all the old currency from circulation. Ackersdijck stated that the introduction of paper money had too often led to catastrophes in other countries. He was also suspicious of the Netherlands Bank which was to store the metal supply until the new currency could be released. He spoke of the Netherlands Bank as the only bank in the world which kept its operations almost entirely secret.[32]

To a large extent Ackersdijck's pamphlet on the currency situation was descriptive, and it did not include much explanation of the author's reasoning and conclusions respecting currency

[30] Jan Ackersdijck, *Nederlands Muntwezen* (Utrecht, 1845), pp. 3–6.
[31] *Ibid.*, pp. 15–18, 31–33.
[32] *Ibid.*, pp. 20–30, 34–35.

legislation. Since Ackersdijck had focused his attention specifically on the Dutch situation, his views were relevant to currency problems at large, only to a limited extent.

W. C. Mees addressed himself to currency problems in a number of his writings, in which he expounded ideas of greater generality than those of Ackersdijck.[33] According to Pierson, Mees was first to set forth the theory of international bimetallism, which has also been associated with the names of such men as Cernuschi, Wolowski, and Courcelle-Seneuil in France, Seyd in England, and Laveleye in Belgium.[34] The germs of Mees' theory of bimetallism were present already in his lectures at "Felix Meritis" in 1852–1853 on "The consequences of an increased supply of precious metals." These lectures, as well as several other papers, were inspired by a leading current event, namely, the gold discoveries in California and Australia in and after 1848. In the above mentioned lectures Mees predicted that, because of the operation of a bimetallic currency standard in France and in other countries, the value of gold would not decline as drastically as was generally anticipated: instead both gold and silver would depreciate to some extent.[35]

In a journal article in 1857 Mees examined the question of "Whether the Dutch had been wise in adopting a silver standard" in 1847. In this paper Mees explained how the existence of a double standard in a number of countries had tempered the depreciation of gold resulting from the gold discoveries. As the value of gold declined, he stated, double-standard countries had replaced part of their silver currency with gold. Thus the demand for gold increased while that for silver decreased, leading to a

---

[33] Mees held three lectures in a scholarly society in Amsterdam, "Felix Meritis," during the winter of 1852–1853 titled "Over de Gevolgen van eene Vermeerderde Voortbrenging der Edele Metalen." Only abstracts of the lectures were published in the Proceedings of "Felix Meritis." Furthermore, Mees published "Eenige Opmerkingen over de Gevolgen der Vermeerderde Voortbrenging van Goud," *Staatkundig en Staathuishoudkundig Jaarboekje*, VII (1855), 302–310; "Hebben wij wel Gedaan, met het Zilver tot eenigen Muntstandaard aan te Nemen?," *Tijdschrift voor Staathuishoudkunde en Statistiek*, XIV (1857), 249–274; "Maatregelen Der Regering Tegen Den Omloop Van Vreemde Munt," *De Economist*, IX (1860), 373–388; and "De Muntstandaard in Verband met de Pogingen tot Invoering van Eenheid van Munt," *Verslagen en Mededeelingen der Koninklijke Akademie van Wetenschappen, Afdeeling Letterkunde*, XII (Amsterdam, 1869), 1–45.

[34] N. G. Pierson, "Levensbericht Van Mr. W. C. Mees," *op. cit.*, p. 345. Also see H. B. Russell, *International Monetary Conferences* (New York, 1898), p. 103.

[35] Pierson, *ibid.*, p. 340.

depreciation of both metals. Since silver had depreciated between three to four per cent less than gold, gold-standard countries had experienced more drastic price increases than had silver-standard countries; accordingly, Mees concluded, the silver standard had been beneficial for Holland, up to that time. He was not certain, however, that the silver standard would continue to be a source of advantage to Holland. In 1857 Mees entertained the possibility that a number of European double-standard countries might convert to a gold standard, with a resulting demonetization of a large amount of silver. Consequently the white metal would depreciate drastically. Mees formulated this possibility in hypothetical terms, but it proved to be an accurate forecast of the currency situation about fifteen years later.[36]

Mees presented his full-fledged theory of international bimetallism in a lecture to the Royal Academy of Sciences in 1869: "The Currency Standard in Connection with Attempts at Establishing Currency Uniformity." The main requirement of a sound metallic currency, said Mees, is stability in the value of the metal. Putting the issue of currency uniformity aside for a moment, Mees suggested that for less developed economies only the silver standard would be suitable, whereas for more advanced economies the gold standard would be preferable, though on balance the degree of superiority of gold to silver was only slight. Mees added that adherence to a monometallic standard could not be combined successfully with international currency uniformity, because of the resulting instability in the value of the metal. As a matter of fact, the only currency standard which, according to Mees, would make international currency uniformity feasible, was the bimetallic standard.[37]

Mees continued to explain that a bimetallic standard was practicable only when adopted by a large number of countries, since this would minimize the fluctuations in market value of the two metals. Mees pointed out the following advantages inherent in international bimetallism: (1) it made currency uniformity feasible; (2) it would provide greater stability in the value of metallic currency than would be possible under alternative arrangements;

[36] W. C. Mees, "Hebben wij wel Gedaan, met het Zilver tot eenigen Muntstandaard aan te nemen?," *op. cit.*, pp. 258–274.

[37] W. C. Mees, "De Muntstandaard in Verband Met De Pogingen Tot Invoering Van Eenheid Van Munt," *op. cit.*, pp. 2–9, 24–34.

and (3) it would make possible the simultaneous circulation of gold and silver, a goal which could not be realized under a bimetallic standard for single countries. To Mees the desirability of currency uniformity rested on certain qualifications. If in the case of a monetary union, strict observance of agreements could not be guaranteed, and if the transmission of maladjustments from one country to others could not be prevented, then the independent regulation of each country's currency would have to be considered preferable.[38]

During the 1860's there was a great deal of discussion in Europe about a uniform world-wide currency system. In 1867 Mees represented Holland at an International currency conference in Paris where he was the only member who voted against the proposal of a universal gold standard. He maintained his position that currency uniformity could only work out under an international bimetallic currency standard. The viewpoint favoring international bimetallism gained popularity among Dutch economists during the last quarter of the century.[39] However, it remained a purely academic scheme, and by the end of the century the idea had lost its force.

The core of Mees' writings on currency questions has been presented. Though he usually addressed himself to Holland's specific problems, his writings reflected a wider interest. In depth of analysis and scope of discussion he surpassed his contemporaries on most issues.

Banking Issues

In the early 1860's banking policy in the Netherlands was the occasion of a number of publications on banking issues. The literature was largely controversial, and most of the leading Dutch economists of the period participated in the discussion. Expiration of the second charter of the Netherlands Bank in the year 1863–1864 set off the controversy, which resembled the Currency-Banking controversy that had taken place in England earlier in the century.

The Netherlands Bank was founded in 1814 as a joint-stock company, and was granted a charter by Willem I for twenty-five

---

[38] *Ibid.*, pp. 10, 31–34, 44.
[39] G. M. Verrijn Stuart, "Honderd Jaar Gold– en Bankwezen," *op. cit.*, p. 890.

years. In 1838 the charter was renewed for another twenty-five years. The seat of the bank was in Amsterdam, and though the decree of 1838 had permitted the foundation of a branch bank in Rotterdam, the Netherlands Bank remained a purely local institution until 1864. Among its other privileges, the bank had a monopoly of note issue. Strictest secrecy concerning the bank's operations had been stipulated in the charter, and was adhered to until 1852 when publicity concerning some of the bank's operations was demanded.

In 1847 a forty per cent metallic reserve was required for the issue of bank notes, and notes were not to exceed the value of 52,000,000 fl. Prior to 1847 no specific requirements regarding the issue and backing of bank notes had been decreed. The volume of credit extended by the bank was extremely moderate at first. This was largely due to the qualms of Dutch businessmen regarding the use of credit.[40]

The bank act of 1863 brought about certain changes. Though the Netherlands Bank was still given exclusive privilege in the issuance of bank notes, Article 1 of the act stated that the establishment of additional issue banks could be authorized. However, this step has never been taken. The act of 1863 also required the establishment of a branch bank in Rotterdam and at least one agency in every province.

In 1863, when renewal of the charter of the Netherlands Bank had to be decided upon, economists debated the issue extensively. Though there was general agreement on the worthiness of the bank's performance, the monopoly position of the bank was seriously questioned. All writers endorsed the existence of a central bank, but different views were expressed in regard to the extent of power and exclusive privilege which should be granted to this institution. The main topics of discussion can be stated as: monopoly versus freedom in the issuance of bank notes; type and amount of regulation required for bank note issue.

Only one economist, N. G. Pierson, fully endorsed the monopo-

---

[40] About the Netherlands Bank see N. G. Pierson, *Leerboek der Staathuishoudkunde*, I, 539–550; Simon Vissering, "De Nederlandsche Bank Gedurende Haar Vijftigjaarig Bestaan" (1863) in *Herinneringen*, III, 44–131; Baasch, *op. cit.*, pp. 559–564; Richard Van Der Borght, "A History of Banking in the Netherlands," in *A History of Banking In All The Leading Nations*, IV (1896), 260–324; G. M. Verrijn Stuart, *Geld, Crediet, en Bankwezen*, II, Vijfde Druk (Wassenaar, 1943), 128–167.

listic position of the Netherlands Bank. Though Pierson did not find himself in complete agreement with either the currency school or the banking school, his position was closer to the former of the two schools. Pierson stated that except during periods of crisis it was in the public interest that a discrepancy between the metallic and note currency be avoided. He also expressed the view that the interest rate was an important determinant of the volume of bank notes and that the banks could thus induce speculation. He therefore concluded that since the banks had a certain amount of control over the amount of note currency in circulation, over issue was possible and dangerous. For this reason Pierson contended that the issuance of bank notes should remain a privilege of the Netherlands Bank exclusively.[41]

Though Pierson rejected most of the ideas which constitute the "banking principle," he attributed to adherents of this doctrine a clearer understanding of the nature of different forms of cerdit than to the currency school theorists. Pierson appreciated that banking school members recognized the interchangeability of bank notes and deposits when they admitted that bank deposits constituted an important part of the circulating medium. The fact that currency school theorists differentiated between bank notes and bank deposits was regarded by Pierson as their most crucial mistake.[42]

Pierson did not refute the supposed fact that bank notes if issued in excess of needed currency would return to the bank. However, the form in which these notes returned to the bank was a crucial factor, ignored by banking school theorists. Pierson pointed out that whether excessive bank notes returned to the bank in the form of debt liquidation or in the form of bank deposits would have decidedly different implications. Not only was the volume of the circulating medium of significance; its composition was equally relevant to the question at hand.[43]

Pierson discussed the monopolistic character of the note-issuing power of the Netherlands Bank. A monopoly is objectionable, stated Pierson, when it provides benefits for a restricted

[41] N. G. Pierson, *De Toekomst Der Nederlandsche Bank* (Haarlem, 1863), pp. 12–43.
[42] *Ibid.*, pp. 18–28. Also Pierson, *Leerboek der Staathuishoudkunde*, I, 500–507.
[43] Pierson, *Leerboek der Staathuishoudkunde*, I, 505–507; Pierson, *De Toekomst Der Nederlandsche Bank*, pp. 28–30.

few; but when monopolistic power is for the benefit of all, the monopolistic institution attains the character of a "police device."[44] A slight change in Pierson's attitude was reflected when in a later work he expressed his approval of Article 1 of the Banking Act of 1863, stating that it was undesirable to exclude decentralized banking on an a priori basis.[45]

The ideas of Vissering were closely related to those of Pierson. Though Vissering insisted on the need for a central bank with exceptional power, he did not believe it necessary that the Netherlands Bank be the only bank entitled to issue notes. In Vissering's opinion; casting the issue into terms of monopoly and competition was to disguise the nature of the basic problem. How the banking system could best supply the amount of credit needed in the economy while at the same time assuring a sound circulating medium was, according to Vissering, a better formulation of the issue. Vissering, as did Pierson, believed that overissue was possible and therefore favored a limited freedom of bank note creation. Vissering drew a distinction between bank notes and other forms of credit and concluded that regulation of bank note issuance alone would provide an adequate check on the money supply. Vissering also admitted that overissue could only take place in the short run, since excess bank notes would flow back to the bank in the long run; he pointed to a time lag between overissue and the symptoms thereof, and stated that this lag could be responsible for serious maladjustments.[46]

If need should arise for additional note-issue banks, besides the Netherlands Bank, Vissering saw no reason why a number of cooperating local banks could not be set up. He demanded that a set of requirements for the founding of new banks should be specified by law, and stated the conditions which he considered essential. Legislative regulation of this sort was justifiable, according to Vissering, because the value of the monetary medium was involved.[47]

Two Dutch economists may be cited who supported the Banking-School viewpoints. Both Otto Van Rees and J. T. Buys believed the needs of business to be the force that controlled the volume

[44] Pierson, *De Toekomst Der Nederlandsche Bank*, pp. 41–43.

[45] Pierson, *Leerboek der Staathuishoudkunde*, I, 544.

[46] Simon Vissering, "Open Brief Over De Bank-Kwestie Aan Den Heer Mr. O. Van Rees," *De Economist*, XII (1863), 373–387, 381.

[47] *Ibid.*, pp. 384–385.

of bank notes. They stated that the banks had no choice in the matter, as they were mere servants of the public. Although they did not question the usefulness of a central bank, both Van Rees and Buys were resolute opponents of the monopolistic character of the Netherlands Bank. They demanded that the privilege of note issue be granted to other banks as well. Though Buys pleaded for freedom limited by certain restrictions, Van Rees, the most radical of all, was a spokesman for complete freedom.[48] Van Rees objected to Vissering's distinction between bank notes and other forms of credit. In his explanation of the interchangeability of different types of credit he referred to Fullarton, Mill and Macleod. He argued that it was of no avail to control only the note issues of banks. Though Van Rees did not deny that banks could occasionally cause harm through overissue, it was his opinion that freedom with inherent dangers had more to offer than regulation which provided security. Thus he stated that a good law regulating joint stock companies combined with obligatory publicity of banking operations would provide a sufficient amount of order in the circulating medium.[49]

In the opinion of Buys, bank notes represented just one of a thousand means to induce speculation; how, therefore, could a limitation of bank note issue dampen speculative activity. Provided certain regulations were made specific and obeyed, Buys favored freedom for banks of issue. He had the following restrictions in mind: (1) permit bank notes only above 25 fl.; (2) stipulate a ratio between specie and note currency; (3) request that a reserve requirement be obeyed; (4) require publicizing of weekly reports on banking operations. The regulations proposed by Buys called forth criticism from both Vissering and Pierson, who judged them to be overly restrictive during normal times and yet insufficiently flexible in periods of crisis, with the result that the general usefulness of banks to the economy would be reduced.[50]

[48] P. Verloren submitted a dissertation on the banking issue at the University of Utrecht in 1864. His position was one resembling that of the banking principle theorists and he demanded as much freedom as did Van Rees. Pierson wrote an extensive review article of Verloren's book. N. G. Pierson, "Vrijheid of Beperking," bespreking van *De Verhouding Van Den Staat Tot Het Bankwezen*, in *Verspreide Economische Geschriften* van Pierson, IV.

[49] Otto Van Rees, "Antwoord Over De Bank-Kwestie Aan Den Heer Mr. S. Vissering," *De Economist*, XII (1863), 448–452.

[50] Pierson, *De Toekomst Der Nederlandsche Bank*, pp. 50–51; Vissering, in *De Economist*, XII (1863), 380.

It might be mentioned that W. C. Mees also advocated central-
ization of bank note issue, but as president of the Netherlands
Bank he did not publish his views on the issue involved in the
controversy. In Pierson's biographical essay on Mees, the influence of Mees on the Dutch banking system and on the banking
act of 1863 were spoken of with high esteem.[51] Vissering also
devoted an article to this phase of Mees' achievement as an
economist.[52] Under the leadership of Mees, the Netherlands Bank,
by means of branch banks and offices spread its activities and
influence on economic life throughout Holland. The bank carried
out its function successfully and discussion of the issue of freedom
versus centralized note issuing power soon became outdated.

Practically all publications which grew out of the currency-
banking controversy in Holland appeared in 1863 or 1864 when
the first Dutch banking act was about to be formulated. Prior to
the appearance of this pressing issue leading Dutch economists
were not prompted to publish on banking questions. The controversy was outstanding in that it incited comments from practically every leading economist of the time. Though the debate was
extremely short-lived and confined to immediately relevant issues,
it called forth explanations of banking operations by Dutch
economists which might otherwise not have been formulated.

Public Finance

When Holland regained her independence in 1813, she was
confronted with a sizable national debt of over 1,232 million fl.
One-third of the debt was floating and the remaining two-thirds
were held in the form of perpetuities. The union with Belgium
enlarged the debt even further, so that annual expenditures on
interest alone amounted to 15.4 million fl. For an impoverished
state such as Holland in the early nineteenth century, a debt of
this magnitude constituted a heavy burden. This burden became
increasingly heavy as the management of the national finances
was carried out in a most irresponsible fashion. As of 1820 government expenditures were in part appropriated on a ten-year basis.
In 1822 a sinking fund was set up, the operations of which ulti-

---

51 Pierson, "Levensbericht Van Mr. W. C. Mees," *op. cit.*, pp. 349–352.
52 Simon Vissering, "De Nederlandsche Bank Onder Het Bestuur Van Mr. W. C.
Mees," in *Verzamelde Geschriften* van Vissering, II, 302–335.

mately increased rather than redeemed the debt. Between 1814 and 1830 the Dutch national debt expanded significantly, and the interest burden grew from 15.4 million fl. in 1814 to nearly 25 million fl. in 1830.[53]

After 1830 the government's financial needs were still pressing, but at that time the colonies began to yield sizable revenues. During the late 1830's average annual profits accruing from the colonies ranged between 10 and 13 million fl.[54] In 1840 the sinking fund was dissolved and secret financial operations by the government were ended. In 1841 the perpetual debt was converted into floating debt in order to make possible more definite estimates of the state's financial requirements. Additional conversion plans were carried out successfully after 1844.[55] Hence, whereas in 1842 payments on the debt amounted to nearly 50 per cent of the budget, after 1844, as a result of a combination of sound financial policy with growing colonial profits, provision was made for a gradual reduction of the debt.[56]

In view of the financial situation described above, it follows that the economy suffered from burdensome taxes. Rising taxes during the first part of the century had apparently been oppressive to trade and industry as well as to the consumer.[57] During the 1840's increasing awareness developed respecting the unsystematic nature of the tax structure. Demands for its liberalization gradually were expressed, and reforms were advocated on grounds of freedom of trade and industry. However, reorganization of the Dutch tax system proceeded much more slowly than had reforms in other areas of economic policy. As a result, unified and methodical fiscal policy was not introduced in Holland until the 1890's.[58]

In the field of public finance writers turned to problems of public expenditures and debt management only infrequently, apparently preferring to deal with problems of taxation. A systematic approach is not to be found in Dutch literature respecting

[53] Baasch, *op. cit.*, pp. 540–550; Brugmans, "De Financieele Crisis van 1844," in *Welvaart en Historie*, pp. 61–74; J. J. Weeveringh, *Handleiding Tot De Geschiedenis Der Staatsschulden*, 1 (Haarlem, 1852).

[54] Brugmans, *ibid.*, p. 64.

[55] Baasch, *op. cit.*, pp. 547–550; Weeveringh, *op. cit.*, p. 214.

[56] Brugmans, "De Financieele Crisis van 1844," *op. cit.*, p. 63.

[57] Baasch, *op. cit.*, p. 550.

[58] *Ibid.*, p. 558.

fiscal problems during the period under consideration. However, during the last two decades of the century analysis of taxation and the national budget made considerable progress.[59]

In this section Ackersdijck's views on the public debt management and on taxation will be considered first. Next there will be a brief presentation of some general views of Dutch economists on taxation. The discussion will also deal with a publication by W. C. Mees on some principles of taxation.

In 1843 Ackersdijck wrote a pamphlet highly critical of the management of Dutch national finances, labeling it unsound, irresponsible, and contrary to sound reasoning.[60] Ackersdijck was disturbed by the fruitlessness of continuously growing expenditures and by imprudent administration of fiscal matters, as a result of which the growth in public debt constantly exceeded the increase in government expenditures. He also objected to the secrecy which surrounded the conduct of governmental finance.

Ackersdijck's publication was occasioned by conversion proposals made in the early 1840's, to which he took strong objection. He criticized these proposals on the ground that they involved carelessness and ambiguous planning, failure to determine the time period within which a proposal was to be carried out, and an attempt to consolidate stocks of different kinds. The basis of these proposals was the disposal of a sum of 80,000,000 fl. which had been the Belgian share of the Dutch national debt. Stocks bearing $4\frac{1}{2}$ and 5 per cent interest were to be converted into stocks yielding 3 per cent. The reason for the high rate of interest on the national debt, stated Ackersdijck, was to be associated with a lack of public confidence. The proposed measures would only diminish the trustworthiness of government loans. Punctuality in interest payments and adequate debt redemption were defined by Ackersdijck as methods best suited to improve the state of public credit. Once this had been achieved, a lowering of interest rates on government loans would become possible.[61]

Conversion plans could only be carried out successfully, explained Ackersdijck, when stock was selling above par. He was not at all convinced that this was the case in Holland. For this reason

[59] C. Goedhart, "Honderd Jaar Openbare Financien," in *De Economist*, C (1952), 958–996.
[60] Jan Ackersdijck, *Nederlands Financieen, – Nationale Schuld* (Amsterdam, 1843).
[61] Ackersdijck, *op. cit.*, pp. 19–28.

Ackersdijck suggested that the available sum of 80 million fl. be applied to redemption of the highest interest paying debt. Owners of 5 per cent stock could then be given the option of having their stock converted. It would thus be tested whether the time was ripe for debt conversion. However, the resumption of public confidence must be a foremost consideration in any debt-administration program.[62] The proposals which Ackersdijck had criticized were not approved in parliament, but new reforms substituted in 1844 included certain conversion schemes which were carried out successfully.

Writings by Dutch economists on the subject of taxation were unsystematic and based on a good deal of arbitrary judgment. Most of the literature on taxation was addressed to changes in specific taxes in isolation rather than to analysis of the tax system in general. Writings of this nature were numerous, but they will not be considered here.

Ackersdijck in a pamphlet written in 1849 discussed the possibilities of raising revenues to cover a 15 million fl. deficit in the national budget.[63] His approach to the subject of taxation was similar to that of most Dutch economists of the time. A property tax was not acceptable to Ackersdijck and he was dubious about income taxes. Instead he recommended a 100 per cent increase in the liquor excise and a reform in the method of taxing sugar. He reasoned that liquor taxes were advisable from a moral viewpoint, and pointed out that though a sugar excise had been in effect for some time, it failed to yield revenues for the government because of its faulty design. Ackersdijck also proposed a tax on coffee and tobacco, since these goods were not looked upon as necessities. He felt confident that the needed sum could thus be collected by the government without imposing an undue burden on anyone concerned.[64] Ackersdijck thus addressed himself to the specific question of raising a certain amount of money in the form of revenues, and in this context examined specific taxes and their yields, but without referring to the Dutch tax system or to general principles of taxation.

A student of Ackersdijck, E. Van Voorthuysen examined the

---

[62] *Ibid..* pp. 29–32.
[63] Jan Ackersdijck, *Over Belastingen en Bezuiniging* (Utrecht, 1849).
[64] *Ibid.*, pp. 18–40.

subject of income taxes in a doctoral dissertation.[65] A detailed examination of the merits and defects of income taxes was presented, in the light of which the author concluded that the income tax entailed excessive interference with privacy, could not be instituted in a manner to insure equal sacrifice, and ought to be resorted to by a government only when there existed no alternatives.[66] This author also discussed the income tax as it had been instituted in other countries, primarily in Britain, and noted the reactions expressed in these countries. His objections to income taxes were based primarily on technicalities and on difficulties attending the practical administration of an income tax. Like most Dutch economists he apparently was not opposed on principle to income taxes.[67]

During the 1840's and 1850's excises were attacked in Holland as being contrary to a liberal tax system. It was mentioned earlier that both Vissering and Buys in their discussion of wages and poverty objected to the tax system because it was too burdensome on the cost of living.[68] But neither of these writers recommended ways of shifting the tax burden. Other economists such as De Bruyn Kops and Van Rees shared the opinion that direct taxes were preferable to indirect ones, and advanced criticisms against consumption taxes in particular.[69] Unfortunately they gave little indication of their reasons for prefering one kind of a tax to another.

A published lecture delivered by W. C. Mees to the Royal Academy of Sciences in 1874 is one of the few Dutch works in which

---

[65] E. Van Voorthuysen, *De Directe Belastingen, Insonderheid Die op de Inkomsten* (Utrecht, 1848).

[66] *Ibid.*, II, 92–99.

[67] Ackersdijck endorsed the views expressed about income taxes by Voorthuysen in *Belastingen en Bezuiniging*, p. 12. Another definite opponent of income taxes was Sloet Tot Oldhuis, see "De Belasting op de Inkomsten," *Tijdschrift voor Staathuishoudkunde en Statistiek*, XXVIII (1875), 176–185. Pierson mentioned Gogel and De Bosch Kemper as additional opponents of income taxes in Holland, see N. G. Pierson, "De In-Komstenbelasting," *Verspreide Economische Geschriften*, V, 23. Pierson himself opposed income taxes on theoretical grounds in the above article. Later in the century there was considerable controversy about income taxes among Dutch economists, see C. Goedhart, "Honderd Jaar Openbare Financien," *op. cit.*, pp. 962–968.

[68] J. T. Buys, "Over Arbeidsloonen," *op. cit.*, and Simon Vissering, "Over Werkloonen en Volksvoeding, *op. cit.*

[69] J. L. De Bruyn Kops, *Beginselen Van Staathuishoudkunde*, II, 350; Otto Van Rees, "De Regeering En De Nijverheid," in *Staatkundig en Staathuishoudkundig Jaarboekje*, XII (1860), 268.

general principles of taxation are treated.[70] Citing certain statements of Adam Smith and John Stuart Mill, Mees pointed out the difference between two principles of equal tax distribution: (1) taxation in accordance whit ability to pay, and (2) taxation in accordance with benefits derived from the state. Either principle, stated Mees, if applied, would result in a tax system decidedly different than would the other. The second part of Mees' paper was devoted to the difference in burden between an old and a new tax. Adjustments take place over time within a society as it responds to taxes. Since a shifting of tax burdens is possible, the effect of a tax may change between the time of its inception and some later period. For this reason Mees inferred that a particular tax structure had more significant effects on the overall economic growth of a society than on the relative well-being of different classes in that society.[71]

A third point made by Mees concerns the fairness of a tax structure. He contended that fairness was only one of several canons of a sound tax system. Equally important were the cost of collection and a minimal discrepancy between sacrifice made and the yield of the tax. If a particular tax structure resulted in a large difference between the amount collected and the revenue placed at the government's disposal, fairness of distribution should perhaps be sacrificed to efficiency in the method of taxation.[72]

HISTORICAL WRITINGS

Dutch economists in the nineteenth century were historically oriented only to a limited extent. Studies on economic history and the history of economic thought were rare during this period, and most economic writers refrained from such research altogether. It is the purpose of this section, therefore, to draw attention to the few economists who did engage in historical investi-

---

[70] W. C. Mees, "Opmerkingen Omtrent Gelijke Verdeeling Van Belasting," *Verslagen en Mededeelingen der Koninklijke Akademie van Wetenschappen*, Afdeeling Letterkunde, V (Amsterdam, 1874).

[71] *Ibid.*, pp. 11–21. Pierson took issue with this point of Mees, if it was to be interpreted to mean that in the course of time taxes lose their undesirable effects. See *Leerboek der Staathuishoudkunde*, II, 501.

[72] W. C. Mees, "Opmerkingen Omtrent Gelijke Verdeeling Van Belasting," *op. cit.*, pp. 21–24.

gations. Writings on the history of economic thought will be examined first, and, then those on economic history.

Among the nineteenth-century Dutch economists previously mentioned in this study, Van Rees showed the greatest interest in history. Before Pierson he was the leading figure among economists in Holland insofar as his work in the history of economic thought is concerned; in fact even until the present, Van Rees is one of very few economists who took an interest in the development of Dutch economic thought. Both his first and his last publication, as well as several others of his works, were devoted to Dutch economic thinking.

In 1851 Van Rees submitted a dissertation at the University of Utrecht on one of the main works by Pieter de la Court, *Aanwijsing der politike gronden en maximen van de Republike van Holland en West-Friesland*, which was designated by Laspeyres as the classic work on this seventeenth-century writer.[73] In 1854 Van Rees won a gold prize with his essay on Van Hogendorp, *Verhandeling Over De Verdiensten Van Gijsbert Karel Van Hogendorp*. Laspeyres has noted that Chapter I of this study on Van Hogendorp represented the best treatment available of Dutch economic thought during the eighteenth century.[74] Van Rees' review of eighteenth-century economics was of course incomplete as he was merely providing background information for his main topic. Nevertheless, he was original in writing about Dutch economic thinkers, and perhaps this realization became an incentive for his later two-volume study on the history of Dutch economics.

Van Rees also gave two inaugural speeches, later published, both of which were concerned with topics in the field of the history of economic thought. In 1858, when he started a teaching position at the University of Groningen, he reviewed the history of Dutch economics from the seventeenth to the nineteenth century in his inaugural address.[75] In 1860, when he was appointed to a chair at the University of Utrecht, he spoke about the development of statistics.[76]

In the 1850's two studies were published by Dutch writers on

[73] Laspeyres, *op. cit.*, p. 52.
[74] *Ibid.*
[75] Otto Van Rees, *Redevoering Over De Staathuishoudkundige Geschiedenis Van Nederland* (Zutphen, 1858).
[76] Otto Van Rees, *Redevoering Over De Wetenschap Der Statistiek* (Utrecht, 1860).

history of economic thought in general, but they devoted only very brief accounts to the development of Dutch economics.[77] In 1859 Wilhelm Roscher suggested to the Jablonowskische Gesellschaft, a scholarly society at Leibzig, that a prize contest should be announced on the economic literature of Holland up to the early eighteenth century. The only response came from Etienne Laspeyres, lecturer of economics and political science at the University of Heidelberg, whose study *Geschichte Der Volkswirtschaftlichen Anschauungen der Niederlaender* was honored with the gold prize in 1863. After Laspeyres' study had been published in German, Van Rees was asked to translate the book into Dutch. However, Van Rees felt that a somewhat different approach from that of Laspeyres would shed additional light on the subject, and he, therefore, decided to write his own version of the early development of Dutch economic thought.[78] Van Rees elaborated on Dutch economic history to a greater extent than Laspeyres had done, and devoted one entire volume of his study to the Dutch colonies and the trading companies. It had been Van Rees' intention to publish a third volume on Dutch economics during the eighteenth century, but his life ended before he could carry out his plan. Until the present time, therefore, the works of Laspeyres and Van Rees remained the only two studies dealing exclusively with the history of pre-nineteenth-century Dutch economic thought.

Literature in the field of economic history is about as limited in volume as the Dutch writings on the history of economic thought. In this area too, Van Rees was one of the most active writers. He contributed to the second edition of a popular work on Dutch history in general. *Algemeene Geschiedenis* (Utrecht, 1854–1859), second edition, 1863. Van Rees also collaborated on volume III of another history of Holland, Arend's *Algemeene Geschiedenis des Vaderlands* (Amsterdam, 1857–1858). It is not certain to what extent his contributions to these works were connected with economics, as one of his biographers, J. A. Fruin, has expressed the

[77] J. A. Molster, *Geschiedenis der Staathuishoudkunde van de Vroegste Tijden tot Heden* (Amsterdam, 1851); E. W. De Rooy, *Geschiedenis der Staathuishoudkunde in Europa* (Amsterdam, 1851). The latter was allegedly a revision of Blanqui's *Histoire de l'Économie Politique*, with supplementation on Dutch economics, see Laspeyres, *op. cit.*, p. 51.

[78] Otto Van Rees, *Geschiedenis der Staathuishoudkunde in Nederland Tot Het Einde Der Achttiende Eeuw*, 2 vols. (Utrecht, 1868).

view that Van Rees' efforts could have been put to better use in his own field.[79] A series of lectures given by Van Rees at "Felix Meritis," a scholarly society in Amsterdam, dealt with the history of Dutch colonial settlements in North America.[80] Practically all of Van Rees' writings were in the field of history, economic history, and history of economic thought. Judged on the basis of his literary activity he probably was more detached from the current issues of his time than were his contemporaries, for he rarely became involved with incidental writings.

Additional works of a historical nature should be mentioned here because they were written by leading Dutch economists during the relevant period. The first published work of W. C. Mees was a historical investigation, the only one of its kind written by Mees. The topic he chose was the history of banking in Holland during the time of the republic.[81] A major part of the study was devoted to the well-known Bank of Amsterdam, and the book is of lasting historical value. In 1847 D. A. Portielje and S. Vissering published a history of British tariff reforms.[82] This work, as mentioned earlier in the present chapter, was designed to stimulate Dutch emulation of British trade policy. For this reason the book was policy-oriented at the same time that it was a historical investigation. So too was De Bosch Kemper's historical investigation of pauperism in Holland, a study inspired by questions relating to government regulation of poor relief.[83]

The impression that no studies were written in the field of economic history between 1800 and 1870 would be erroneous. Certainly there were books published on such subjects as the history of shipping, fishing, trade, industry, and other economic topics. However, it is true that leading Dutch economists of the period under consideration did not frequently turn to historical research, and that they demonstrated little interest in the history of economic thought.

---

[79] J. A. Fruin, "Levensbericht van Mr. Otto Van Rees," *op. cit.*, pp. 133–134.

[80] Otto Van Rees, *Geschiedenis der Nederlandsche Volksplantingen in Noord-Amerika, Beschouwd Uit Het Oogpunt Der Koloniale Politiek* (Tiel, 1855).

[81] W. C. Mees, *Proeve Eener Geschiedenis Van Het Bankwezen In Nederland Gedurende Den Tijd Der Republiek* (Rotterdam, 1838).

[82] D. A. Portielje and Simon Vissering, *Geschiedenis Der Tariefhervorming in Engeland* (Amsterdam, 1847).

[83] J. De Bosch Kemper, *Geschiedkundig Onderzoek Naar De Armoede In Ons Vaderland*, (Haarlem, 1851).

THEORETICAL WRITINGS

Economic theory was incorporated to a varying extent in the policy-oriented writings of nineteenth-century Dutch economists. The present section has been reserved for purely theoretical literature, or publications which were not motivated by the necessity of solving immediately practical problems. As will be evident from the division of space in this chapter only a relatively small amount of effort was allocated by Dutch economists to non-applied economic theory. For the purpose at hand, textbooks on principles of economics written by Dutch economists will be included in this category of writings.

In 1850 De Bruyn Kops published the first Dutch textbook in economics, a two-volume work called "Principles of Economics" (*Beginselen Van Staathuishoudkunde*). Although this book was highly elementary and tended to evade complex and unresolved theoretical issues, it fulfilled an important function in the early stages of the development of economics in Holland. Vissering wrote a second textbook, "Handbook of Practical Economics" (*Handboek Van Praktische Staathuishoudkunde*), published in 1860–1861, in which the different fields of economics were covered more thoroughly and systematically than in De Bruyn Kops' book. From the style of Vissering's writing it is evident that the book was intended as an outline for the teaching of economic principles. In summary fashion he set forth numerous topics without penetrating into them. Although the book had a practical orientation, it included a good deal of theoretical matter. Neither of these two works is theoretical in the usual sense of the word. They are mentioned here because they represent literary efforts of Dutch economists which were not directly related to applied economics.

It has been indicated previously that Mees' policy-oriented writings were usually more theoretical and wider in scope than those of his contemporaries. By and large it may be stated that Mees was the only one among the group of economists here considered, who was drawn into the field fo pure theory. One of his lectures delivered to the Royal Academy of Sciences in 1877 and subsequently printed in the Proceedings was an "Attempt at Clarification of Some Concepts of Economics."[84] In this lecture value and wealth were the two concepts which Mees had singeld out for clarification. He took issue with Jevons' substitution of utility for the concept of value. Utility, stated Mees, refers to the quality of a good to serve as a means to an end. However, a good may be valued not because it is a means to an end but because it is desired in its own right. Value in this sense would be excluded from the Jevonian concept of utility. Therefore, stated Mees, if the concept of value is to be replaced, a new concept more comprehensive than utility is required.[85] Mees further objected to the ambiguity connected with the concept of wealth as ordinarily used in economics. The usual meaning attached to the concept of wealth denoted the ability of disposing of goods endowed with exchange value. In Mees' opinion the concept of wealth, if so interpreted, placed too much emphasis on ownership whereas wealth should refer to what he called "acquisition potential" (verkrijgingsgelegenheid) as well. It is not entirely clear what Mees had in mind by "acquisition potential." At any rate Mees criticized the concept of wealth as used by economists and found it too delimiting. It is doubtful that Mees contributed to the clarification of the concepts of value and wealth, but he was the only Dutch economist of the period who demonstrated a concern for problems of purely conceptual nature.

Mees' chief work on pure theory was his "Overview of Several Main Topics of Economics" (*Overzicht Van Eenige Hoofdstukken der Staathuishoudkunde*), published in 1866. Concerned about the influence of such economists as Carey, MacLeod and Bastiat, Mees wished to restate some basic economic laws formulated by the classical school, which were in his mind as reputable as general laws in natural science.[86] His book was divided into three parts: production, income distribution, and distribution among different economies. Part two is the most elaborate by far. The investigation proceeded on a very high level of abstraction so that

[84] W. C. Mees, "Poging Tot Verduidelijking Van Eenige Begrippen In De Staathuishoudkunde," *Verslagen en Mededeelingen der Koninklijke Akademie van Wetenschappen*, Afdeeling Letterkunde, VII (Amsterdam, 1877).

[85] *Ibid.*, pp. 11–19.

[86] W. C. Mees, *Overzicht Van Eenige Hoofdstukken Der Staathuishoudkunde* (Amsterdam, 1866), see Preface.

even the illustrations were exempt from any concrete detail.

It would be impossible briefly to review so concentrated a study as Mees' "Overview," especially since it covers a wide theoretical territory. Mees elaborated on the meaning of scarcity, division of labor and economic cooperation; on time involved in the production process, saving as a basis of capital formation, and the limitedness and exhaustibility of natural resources. He outlined conceivable economic imbalances such as the ratio of capital to labor, of circulating to fixed capital, of skilled to unskilled labor. He posed the population problem in the context of resource limitations. He described the competitive price mechanism and later extended it to distribution theory and international trade. Though he refrained from citations and references to other economists, he did not claim to present novel ideas or an original subject matter. His motivation for writing the book was to get rid of the reputation of economics as a "dismal science" and to reinforce the search for economic lawfulness. The moralistic theme of some of his other writings pervaded this book as well, namely that the fruitfulness of resource allocation and the adequacy of income distribution were conditional upon overall intellectual and moral advancement of humanity.

The high level of abstraction which characterizes the "Overview" makes it unique in the Dutch economic literature of the time. Reviewers left the book practically unmentioned in the journals except for an extensive review article by De Bruyn Kops published in *De Economist*, in which he speaks of Mees with a great deal of admiration.[87] Though Mees' "Overview" was not translated into foreign languages, it was discussed by Luigi Cossa in *An Introduction To The Study Of Political Economy*, and according to Pierson it was also mentioned by Achille Loria in his book on rent.[88] Until the last quarter of the nineteenth century, the time of Pierson and his contemporaries, Mees was the dominant figure in theoretical economics in Holland.

---

[87] J. L. De Bruyn Kops, "De Verdeeling Van Den Maatschappelijken Rijkdom," *De Economist* (Het Bijblad, 1867), pp. 382–408).

[88] Luigi Cossa, *An Introduction To The Study Of Political Economy* (London, 1893), pp. 434–435; N. G. Pierson, "Economisch Overzicht," in *Verspreide Economische Geschriften*, II, 502.

GENERALIZATIONS CONCERNING THE NATURE
OF DUTCH ECONOMIC THOUGHT

In this chapter we have discussed the major writings of a group of representative Dutch nineteenth-century economists. On the basis of these writings certain inferences may be made about the nature of Dutch economic thought during the period under consideration.

It was found that Dutch economic writings were concentrated in the following fields of economics: population and pauperism, commercial policy, currency and banking issues, and public finance. For the purpose of this study publications on the corn laws were held to be representative of writings on commercial policy in general. Such areas of inquiry as labor, economic fluctuations, and industrial organization, for example, dit not receive attention by Dutch economists until the late nineteenth and early twentieth century.

A heavy emphasis on applied economics and a relative neglect of economic theory have also been noted. Policy-oriented writings were more numerous by far than historical and theoretical writings. It follows that essentially theoretical analysis was usually neglected in the economic fields of concern to Dutch economists. With the exception of W. C. Mees, not one of the representative figures dealt with price, value, or distribution theory, or with problems of conceptual or methodological nature. Mees was outstanding, furthermore, in that he incorporated far more theoretical analysis into his policy-oriented writings than did any of his contemporaries.

The most outstanding figure among representative Dutch nineteenth-century economists other than Mees, was Otto Van Rees. Van Rees was unusual for a different reason, however, being remembered mainly because of his decidedly historical orientation. Though his contemporaries demonstrated little interest in economic history or in the history of economic thought, most of Van Rees' writings were in these two areas.

By and large, Dutch economists during most of the nineteenth century were interested primarily in applied economics. Furthermore, their practical interests were restricted to specific economic problems faced by the Dutch economy. Whence nineteenth-century Dutch economic literature continued to reflect in large measure an orientation similar to that prominent in seventeenth- and eighteenth-century writings; in particular much of it remained incidental in character. In general, furthermore, the composition of nineteenth-century Dutch economic literature resembled that of the set of economic problems of main concern to the Dutch economic community.

Continuity in nineteenth-century Dutch economic thought was governed by the practical nature of its subject matter. To the extent that economic issues remained unresolved over long periods, one might have expected a continuous preoccupation with these issues to be manifest in the economic literature of the period. This was not always the case, however. Currency-standard problems, for example, though of great importance to the Dutch economy during most of the period covered, were discussed only infrequently and then by but two of the representative group of economists under consideration, namely, Ackersdijck and Mees. In contrast, trade policy and the problem of pauperism, were discussed by most economists and remained subjects of extensive discussion throughout most of the century. Banking problems, however, though of concern to practically all leading economists, were discussed mainly in the course of a very brief period. In sum, therefore, inasmuch as nineteenth-century Dutch economic writings were oriented toward practical issues and since no schools of economic thought developed at Dutch universities, such conti-origin primarily in the continuity of the problems faced by the Dutch economy and hence of concern to at least some Dutch economists.

Dutch economic thought during the nineteenth century was largely eclectic. With the exception of Mees' theory of international bimetallism, it was not marked by originality. The eclecticism of Dutch economists will be examined further in the following chapter.

CHAPTER VII

THE IMPACT OF FOREIGN SCHOOLS ON DUTCH ECONOMIC THOUGHT

The present chapter will deal with the foreign impacts on Dutch economic thought during the nineteenth century. It will be divided into two parts. Brief illustrations of Dutch economic thought during the seventeenth and eighteenth centuries willbe presented in Part I, and a review of foreign influences on Dutch economists during the nineteenth century will constitute Part II. The chapter will be concluded with some generalizations concerning foreign impacts on Dutch economic thought.

An attempt to trace the influence of foreign economists on Dutch economic thought must be confined to purely literary tests, such as for example: (1) an examination of the extent to which Dutch economists were familiar with foreign economic literature and made use of the ideas and concepts of foreign writers to support their own reasoning; and (2) an examination of Dutch translations of foreign economic literature and possibly the motivation for such translations. Unfortunately no statistics are available of the sale and library circulation of foreign economic works or their Dutch translations. It will be necessary to assume, therefore, that the mere event of a translation and reviews as well as citations of foreign economic works by Dutch economists are indicative of an interest in the ideas of respective foreign authors.

These literary tests, however, although they yield a certain type of information, do not eliminate the difficulties involved in evaluating the influence of ideas of a particular writer on a specific course of thought. There still remain such problems as, for example, how much weight should be given to the foreign ideas which were cited and what role should be assigned to attitudes prevalent in the receiving country thus determining its susceptibility to particular trends of thought. In some instances the available information is too limited to permit meaningful generalizations about foreign influences on a particular economist or on nineteenth-century Dutch thought in general. Thus it will be difficult to interpret which trend or trends of foreign thinking tended to overshadow competing schools of thought. On the whole it becomes evident that Dutch economists displayed little sense of self-sufficiency during the nineteenth century, as they appear to have been more inclined to absorb the developments in economic science of other countries than they were to compose a body of economic knowledge on their own.

BRIEF ILLUSTRATIONS OF DUTCH ECONOMIC THOUGHT DURING THE SEVENTEENTH AND EIGHTEENTH CENTURIES

The Dutch were not prolific as far as scholarly economic writings were concerned during the seventeenth and eighteenth centuries. The economic literature of the Netherlands during this period consisted largely of pamphlets, prize essays, dissertations, and, to use Laspeyres' term, "Gelegenheitsschriften," or writings which were motivated by specific events of the day. In contradistinction to economic doctrines in other countries, the Dutch writings were often anonymous, and in those instances where the writer was identified, it usually was not a name which carried reputation or authority. Laspeyres has demonstrated throughout his detailed study that the importance of seventeenth- and eighteenth-century Dutch economics was to be sought not in economic treatises but in the incidental pieces of economic literature.[1] Nevertheless, there were a few selected figures who became more deeply involved with questions of economics than did the numerous pamphleteers. Though these figures are few and far between and though their writings provide little continuity in economic thinking, their views have usually been chosen to depict the nature of Dutch economic thought prior to the nineteenth century.

[1] Laspeyres, *op. cit.*; see Preface of book.

Pre-nineteenth-century Dutch economics has received attention in the literature and will for the greater part be left outside the scope of this study.[2] However, a summary of the main ideas which constituted landmarks in the history of Dutch economic thought supplies perspective of the pre-liberal antecedence of nineteenth-century economists. Pieter de la Court (1618–1685) will be considered as the representative of seventeenth-century economics, and Elias Luzac (1723–1803) and Friedrich Pestel (1724-1803) of the generation just preceding the first nineteenth century economists.

Historians of economic thought have usually linked the long tradition of free trade thinking in Holland to the commercial orientation of the Dutch economy. On the policy level laissez faire was expedient as a method of enhancing activity in direct and intermediate trading functions. During the sixteenth and seventeenth centuries, government in Holland was strongly dominated by merchant regents who constituted the free trade party. The merchants' ideas and interests were of fundamental significance to policy formation and consequently these ideas were also embraced by scholarly and non-scholarly economic literature. As Van Rees has stated, early Dutch theorizing about economic problems was simply inspired by and founded on solutions which had already been put into practice. It appeared to Van Rees that scholars at that time were far removed from being instigators of economic policy measures, and that their writings were most aptly described as vindications of already existing precepts and practices.[3] Thus liberal economic thinking was dominant in the literature and is said to have reflected primarily established policy practices and the merchant ideology.

It cannot be ignored, however, that the Dutch free trade orientation was different from the laissez faire doctrine ex-

---

[2] Laspeyres, *op. cit.*; Otto Van Rees, *Geschiedenis der Staathuishoudkunde in Nederland tot het Einde der Achttiende Eeuw* (Utrecht, 1865); Otto Van Rees, *Redevoering over de Staathuishoudkundige Geschiedenis Van Nederland* (Zutphen, 1858); Otto Van Rees, *De Verdiensten Van Gijsbert Karel Van Hogendorp*, Chapter I; E. W. De Rooy, *Geschiedenis der Staathuishoudkunde in Europa* (Amsterdam, 1851); Siegfried Polak, *Beknopte Geschiedenis Der Staathuishoudkunde in Theorie En Praktijk* (Groningen, 1919); L. J. Zimmerman, *Geschiedenis van het Economisch Denken* (Amsterdam, 1947); H. W. C. Bordewijk, *Theoretisch-Historische Inleiding Tot De Economie* (Den Haag, 1931); P. A. Diepenhorst, *Leerboek Van De Economie*, vol. I, *Geschiedenis Der Economie* (Zutphen, 1946).

[3] Otto Van Rees, *Geschiedenis der Staathuishoudkunde in Nederland*, p. 281.

pounded by Adam Smith and his followers. Free trade was advocated when it served to promote the interests of the merchants; not because it suggested a way of maximizing efficiency and social well being. Frequently conflict broke out even among merchants about the degree of liberalism that was desirable, for not all merchants were in favor of complete laissez faire all the time. In short, the Dutch were not free traders in principle, but the merchants, divided into local groups with particularistic interests, favored a liberal trade policy whenever such a policy appeared to be pragmatic.[4]

Pieter de la Court, it is generally agreed upon, was Hollands' most outstanding pre-nineteenth-century economist. Although his keen insights were developed primarily in response to peculiarly Dutch circumstances his crowning reputation is also based on his widespread influence outside the Netherlands. De la Court was the son of a cotton manufacturer in Leiden, and was trained by his father to become a partner in the business. However, before he devoted himself to the manufacturing of cottons he obtained a degree of law at the University of Leiden.[5]

Somehow he became one of the few seventeenth-century economic writers who failed to endorse every aspect of Dutch economic institutions and policy. However, what makes him such a well-chosen representative is a combination of ideas most typical of Dutch economic thought during the seventeenth century, namely a combination that reflected vacillation between laissez faire and mercantillistic ideas. Although the most vigorous Dutch free-trader of the century, de la Court did not refrain from endorsing several mercantilistic ideas in his writings.[6]

Both Laspeyres and Van Rees found de la Court's ideas to be partially anticipatory of Adam Smith. Among those of de la Court's ideas leading to this interpretation the following stand out: he emphasized freedom to work (what, how, where, and to what purpose) and freedom of occupation in general; he denounced all monopolies, especially the guilds and trading companies; he advocated free competition, believing it more likely to insure the best quality of merchandise and the lowest

⁴ Laspeyres, *op. cit.*, pp. 162–163.
⁵ Otto Van Rees, *Geschiedenis der Staathuishoudkunde in Nederland*, p. 285.
⁶ *Ibid.*, p. 362; Laspeyres, *op. cit.*, p. 166; and Bordewijk, *op. cit.*, p. 176.

prices than was government intervention in industry; he considered a low interest rate, dense population, and the splitting of inheritances to be stimulating to entrepreneurship, and thought of high import and export duties as interfering with trade and industry. On the other hand, de la Court was impressed with the significance of the role of exports as compared to that of domestic consumption in enhancing a country's wealth, and he suggested retaliation in the event of discriminatory import duties when introduced by other countries. He also subscribed to the view that an increase in wealth of one country would necessarily be at the expense of another, and he regarded the taxing of foreign goods as essential when they were in competition with domestic products, even though foreign merchandise often entered the country only to be promptly re-exported. These brief statements do not do justice to de la Court's three main works, in which he expressed his views on economic questions, but they roughly exemplify his approach to economic questions.[7] In the opinion of Van Rees the inconsistency of de la Court regarding freedom of trade did not detract from the significance of his ideas. A product of his age, de la Court did not turn out to be wholly cosmopolitan in his laissez faire attitudes, and he could not refrain from supporting certain mercantilistic opinions.

It should be mentioned that partly for political reasons, de la Court exerted no influence in Holland on practical measures or economic thinking in his time or in the century that followed. It was not until the nineteenth century in fact that the writings of de la Court were re-discovered and appreciated.[8] A number of

[7] *Het Welvaaren der Stadt Leyden*, 1659; *Interest van Holland ofte Gronden van Hollands-Welvaren* (Amsterdam, 1662); *Aanwijsing der heilsame politike Gronden en Maximen van de Republike van Holland en West-Vriesland*, 1669.

[8] In 1851, Van Rees wrote a dissertation: *Verhandeling over de Aanwijsing der politike Gronden en Maximen van Pieter de la Court*; in 1845 B. W. Wttenwaall published in Leiden an introduction and comments to the first publication of a manuscript written in 1659, *Proeve uit een onuitgegeven staathuishoudkundige geschrift, Het Welvaeren der Stad Leyden*, door Mr. Pieter de la Court; in 1825 De Bruyes published *Verhandeling over de staathuishoudkundige waarde van het werk genaamd Aanwijsing ...*, in De Staar (1825), pp. 313–; G. M. Wttenwaall (father of the above) wrote on Pieter de la Court in *Bijdragen tot de Staathuishoudkunde en Statistiek* (Utrecht, 1836), I, 1–52, 376–399; and Sloet Tot Oldhuis discussed de la Court in *Tijdschrift voor Staathuishoudkunde en Statistiek* (1850), VI, 107–, 409–; Sloet claimed in this article that Adam Smith must have been familiar with de la Court's works and adopted some of de la Court's ideas.

Despite the provincial scope of de la Court's writings, his works were widely translated. The *Interest van Holland ofte Gronden van Hollands-Welvaren* (1662)

studies were published on de la Court in the nineteenth century, and one Dutch economist, Sloet Tot Oldhuis, went so far as to claim that Adam Smith had plagiarized some of de la Court's ideas. Smith never indicated that he had been familiar with de la Court and other Dutch economists refuted the claim made by Sloet Tot Oldhuis.

Mercantilism never found as elaborate expression in Holland as it did in many other European countries, at least not as a comprehensive system of ideas for fostering the development and the protection of industry. Yet if a period is to be singled out as one during which certain mercantilistic ideas were more relevant to the Dutch situation than during any other period, the eighteenth century would be selected.[9] The eighteenth century, succeeding the Dutch Golden Age, was one of gradual decline which had culminated in serious economic contraction by the end of the century. Increased competition of foreign markets, shrinkage in the carrying trade, slackening entrepreneurship and declining industry were responsible for stronger emphasis on protective measures and an expanding role of the state.

Mercantilistic ideas can be found in the works of such writers as Friedrich Wilhelm Pestel (1724–1803) and Elias Luzac (1723–1803), even after the publication of Adam Smith's *Wealth of Nations*. Pestel, for example, defended the importance of a favorable trade balance for Holland, agreed that guilds should be maintained since they could promote industry more effectively than alternative agencies, and favored maintaining the trading companies. He also supported the ideas that an increase in trade of one country must result in a diminution of the trade of another country, and suggested that opening the colonies to free trade

received two German translations in 1665 and a third in 1668. In 1671 de la Court's *Aanwijsing der heilsame politike Gronden en Maximen van de Republike van Holland en West-Vriesland* (1669) was translated into German and in 1709 it received a French translation which was published under the title of *Memoires de Jean de Witt, grand pensionnaire de Hollande*. In 1743 an English translation of the same work appeared in which authorship was also attributed to Johan de Witt. See Van Rees, *Geschiedenis der Staathuishoudkunde in Nederland*, pp. 371–372; also Laspeyres, *op. cit.*, pp. 304–306. On grounds of these translations one might suppose that de la Court may have influenced economic thinking in other countries before his ideas affected his own countrymen. It was not until the nineteenth century that works on the history of Dutch economic thought assigned to de la Court the role of a pioneer in the early history of economics.

[9] Van Rees, *Geschiedenis der Staathuishoudkunde in Nederland*, pp. 304,398.

might cut into the large profits derived from that source by the Dutch merchants. Pestel is known also for his views on taxation; he believed that all classes must be taxed and that exemptions and premiums should be granted only in very special circumstances, perhaps because he supposed that a tax on necessities would not put as much pressure on the lower classes as was generally assumed.[10] Luzac's book *Hollands Rijkdom* became a standard work on the development of trade and industry in Holland and gained widespread popularity mainly on grounds of historical description. In volume IV of his work he presented a list of twenty-four recommendations for revivifying the Dutch economy. He suggested reduction of the tax burden on shipping, trading and manufactures, adding that taxes could be increased on luxuries and property. He proposed the establishment of a limited free port; special benefits and premiums for manufacturers; freedom of settlement for industries in rural areas; encouragement of the consumption of domestically produced goods; promotion of education; a strong naval power for defense and protection of shipping, trade and the colonies. Luzac was not adverse to monopolistic institutions such as the guilds and trading companies, but he disagreed with those who emphasized commerce as the exclusive source of wealth, and he stated that navigation and commerce tend to enrich certain inhabitants rather than to enrich the nation at large, whereas fisheries, manufactures, and refining industries necessarily contribute to the wealth of the entire country.[11]

It is evident that the late eighteenth-century writers cited above subscribed in some measure to mercantilist views. This is true also of Adriaan Kluit (1735–1806), who has been classified as a nineteenth-century figure earlier in this study, mainly because of his impact upon the teaching of economics and statistics at Dutch universities in the nineteenth century (see chapters IV and V). In this chapter, however, we will discuss Kluit as a contemporary of Pestel and Luzac since Kluit's economic ideas belong essentially in the pre-liberal phase of Dutch economic thought. It should be noted that Kluit took a more extreme

---

[10] Laspeyres, *op. cit.*, pp. 41–42; Van Rees on Van Hogendorp, *op. cit.*, pp. 48, 54. Pestel's economic ideas were expressed in *Commentarii de republica Batava* (1795).

[11] Elias Luzac, *Hollands Rijkdom*, IV (Leyden, 1783), 531–533; Van Rees on Van Van Hogendorp, *op. cit.*, pp. 42–43; Laspeyres, *op. cit.*, pp. 37–38.

position in his proposals of protectionistic measures than had been taken by his contemporaries Pestel and Luzac; direct cameralistic influence can be found in Adriaan Kluit's writings.

Kluit addressed himself to economic questions mostly during the latter part of his life when he became interested in the teaching of economics and statistics.[12] Kluit's manuscripts apparently included a number of references to foreign economists with whose writings he had been familiar. Kluit stated explicitly that in his statistics course he followed the approach of Achenwall who had been lecturing about economic and political conditions at the University of Goettingen, in the German language since 1749. Among the foreign economists cited by Kluit in his manuscripts were the following: Sueszmilch, Luder, Gentz, Von Justi, Smith, Condillac, and Verri. The last three economists were cited only from the Dutch translations of their writings. Unless Kluit had also read *The Wealth of Nations* in English he could not have been thoroughly familiar with Adam Smith, since the Dutch translation of *The Wealth of Nations* included Book I, chapters 1–10 only.[13]

According to Van Rees Kluit considered Von Justi his favored economist. However, both Van Rees and Vissering were amazed

---

[12] Kluit's views on economic issues were formulated in a book *Iets over Nederlands Koophandel, groei, verval, en herstel* (1794). Inability to locate this book in the Dutch libraries forces us to rely on Van Rees' treatment of it in his book on Van Hogendorp, *op. cit.*, pp. 46–48. Two articles on two unpublished manuscripts of Kluit, which presumably included the content of his course on economic and statistics, yield additional information regarding Kluit's thinking: F. N. Sickenga, "Staathuishoudkunde in het begin der negentiende eeuw hier te lande," *Tijdschrift voor Staathuishoudkunde en Statistiek*, XXVI (1866), 165–175, and Otto Van Rees, "Het Collegie van Adriaan Kluit Over de Statistiek Van Nederland," *Tijdschrift voor Staathuishoudkunde en Statistiek*, XII (1855), 245–263. About Kluit see also Matthys Siegenbeek, *Geschiedenis der Leidsche Hoogeschool*, 1 (Leiden, 1829), 316–368.

[13] Kluit had also referred to such authors as Peuchet, S. Richard, Raynal, and Necker. See Van Rees, "Het Collegie van Adriaan Kluit Over De Statistiek Van Nederland," *op. cit.*, pp. 240–251: Luder, *Ueber Nationalindustrie und Staatswirtschaft* (Berlin, 1800); Von Justi, *Staatswirtschaft* (1755); Sueszmilch, *Die Goettliche Ordnung* (1742); Gentz, *Essai sur l'état actuel de l'administration des finances et de la richesse nationale de la Grande Bretagne* (1800); Peuchet, *Statistique elementaire de la France* (1803); S. Richard, *Traite general du commerce* (1781); Raynal, *Histoire philosophique et politique des etablissements des Europeens dans les deux Indes* (Geneve, 1780); A. Smith, *The Wealth of Nations*, translated by D. Hoola Van Nooten (1796) (Naspeuringen Over De Natuur in Oorzaaken Van Den Rijkdom Der Volkeren), Eerste Deel, Eerste Stuk, Amsteldam; De Condillac, *Koophandel en Staatsbestuur*, translated by D. Hoola Van Nooten (Utrecht, 1782); De Verri, *De Staethundige Oeconomie*, translated from the French edition of "Meditazioni sulla Economia Politica" ((Leiden, 1801). Van Rees claimed that D. Hoola Van Nooten was also responsible for the translation of Verri.

that the works of Smith and Verri did not influence Kluit more strongly.[14] Since Kluit had been under the influence of German cameralism it is possible that he embodied the same "cameralistic resistance to Smith" which Melchior Palyi found in many early nineteenth-century German economists.[15] Palyi had pointed out that cameralist professors often tended to disregard the appearance and content of *The Wealth of Nations*.

Kluit's economic views clearly reflect cameralistic thinking. Kluit divided commercial activity into three distinct operations, importing, exporting, and the carrying trade; he emphasized the last especially. Because he believed that Holland's most important exports were derived from colonial goods, Kluit advocated excluding foreign countries from the Dutch colonial trade, so that this particular source of wealth might be fostered. It seemed to him that allowing the colonies to trade freely with all nations would have disastrous effects on the Dutch economy.

Kluit also claimed that a country could trade profitably only when exports exceeded imports, so that a surplus of money would enter the country. However, Kluit questioned at times whether the trade balance of a country could be regarded as a true indicator of the industriousness and wealth of its economy. The fact that he raised this question indicates that there must have been some doubt in Kluit's mind in regard to this issue, but he never managed to resolve the question. Although he had stated that he believed a nation's wealth to consist primarily in the supply of precious metals, he pointed out in a different context that the true and original source of a nation's wealth was derived not from the supply of money but from the land's and the people's productivity.[16] Thus Kluit had ambivalent feelings regarding the importance which should be attached to the trade balance of a country and regarding the role of the supply of precious metals in determining the wealth of a nation.

Kluit attached far more importance to industry than to agriculture, for agriculture could not create a large demand for labor.

---

[14] Van Rees, "Het Collegie van Adriaan Kluit Over De Statistiek Van Nederland," *op. cit.*, pp. 260–262; Simon Vissering, "De Statistiek Aan De Hoogeschool," *De Gids* (1877), No. 11, p. 2.

[15] Melchior Palyi, "The Introduction of Adam Smith on the Continent," in *Adam Smith, 1776–1926* Chicago, 1926), pp. 192–197.

[16] Van Rees, "Het Collegie van Adriaan Kluit Over De Statistiek Van Nederland," *op. cit.*, p. 255.

On the other hand, he considered industry of extreme importance to an economy, since industry was capable of absorbing many more hands than agriculture, and for this reason industries should be supported and protected by the state. Among the industry-favoring stimuli proposed by Kluit are the following: obligatory consumption of domestic goods by civil servants and the military population; differential duties in the colonies favoring Dutch imports; the raising of duties on foreign, competing goods with the objective of spending the revenues on premiums to industry; doing away with the guilds where ever they had proven harmful to industry; improved care for the poor, particularly with regard to finding employment for them and barring immigrants from the country.[17] It was Kluit's opinion that import and export duties should be regarded as instruments of the state, for the direction of trade into the most profitable channels. Kluit did not object to the investment of savings in foreign countries, as he considered it desirable that the individual remain free to invest where opportunities appeared most lucrative.[18]

Inconsistencies in Kluit's views have been pointed out by Van Rees and by Sickenga in their discussions of Kluit's manuscripts and lecture notes on economics and statistics. In the present chapter our main interest lies in the fact that Kluit was familiar with German cameralists as well as with British and Italian liberal economic thought. Both tendencies influenced Kluit's views but it seems appropriate to classify him with the pre-liberal Dutch economic writers of the late eighteenth century.

FOREIGN INFLUENCES ON DUTCH ECONOMISTS
DURING THE NINETEENTH CENTURY

Nineteenth-century Dutch economists were influenced primarily by liberal trends of economic thought developed in foreign countries. The foreign impact on Dutch economic thought will be presented in the following order: first a group of Dutch economists who were oriented predominantly toward British economic

[17] Sickenga, op. cit., pp. 169–171.
[18] Van Rees, "Het Collegie van Adriaan Kluit Over De Statistiek Van Nederland," op. cit., pp. 256–259.

thought will be discussed. This group consisted of H. W. Tydeman
Jan Ackersdijck, Otto Van Rees, and W. C. Mees. Subsequently
attention will be focused on a second group of Dutch economists,
more eclectic than the former group, and consisting of economists
who were influenced by British, French, and sometimes by
German trends of economic thought as well. Such figures as
Simon Vissering, J. L. De Bruyn Kops, and B. W. A. E. Sloet
Tot Oldhuis constitute the second group of Dutch economists.

H. W. Tydeman (1778–1863) was the first nineteenth-century
Dutch economist who demonstrated a strong interest in British
economic thought. Tydeman's role in transmitting foreign economic thought to Holland was twofold: he continued Kluit's
emphasis on the Achenwall type of statistics; and he was also
responsible for a number of Dutch translations of British works
on liberal economics.

Tydeman may be regarded as a partial follower of Kluit. He
had attended at least one of the courses on economics and statistics given by Kluit at the University of Leiden. Subsequently
Tydeman carried on Kluit's teaching at Leiden, and this perpetu-
ated Kluit's emphasis on the Achenwall type of statistics. Tydeman even provided the Dutch with a book on statistics in
this tradition, when he translated and edited August Von
Schloezer's *Theorie Der Statistiek of Staats-kunde* in 1814.[19] On
the other hand, Tydeman did not support the cameralistic views
of Kluit, endorsing instead liberal economic views, especially
those of British origin.

Tydeman's literary contributions consisted primarily of prize
essays and of prefaces to Dutch translations of foreign economics
books. Although he had planned at one time to write a general
study on "The Economics and Statistics of the Netherlands"
there is no evidence that Tydeman ever got around to the proposed study. Most information regarding Tydeman's economic
views was found in the prefaces to translations which carried his
name.

Tydeman's interests in foreign economics were directed primarily towards England. With the exception of Von Schloezer's
book, all the foreign economics works which Tydeman introduced

---

[19] See Simon Vissering, "De Statistiek Aan De Hoogeschool," *op. cit.*, p. 5. Von
Schloezer was a professor at the University of Goettingen and a disciple of Achenwall.

to the Dutch public were of British origin: A. and P. W. Alison, *A Justification and Evaluation of Provision for the Poor by the State*; N. W. Senior, *Principles of Political Economy*; Mrs. Marcet's *Conversations on Political Economy*; as well as her *John Hopkins' Notions on Political Economy* (all cited in Chapter V). Tydeman mentioned in one of his prefaces that he was also engaged in a translation of McCulloch's *A discourse on the rise, progress, peculiar objects, and importance of political economy*, but as far as is known to the present writer this translation never came into being. Tydeman also mentioned that he had in hand the complete translation of *The Wealth of Nations* as completed by Hoola Van Nooten, who had succeeded in publishing only the first part of Book I in 1796, in the Dutch language. In 1825 Tydeman stated that he was anxious to get the remainder of this translation published and that he was searching for a publisher willing to undertake this project.[20] Despite Tydeman's enthusiasm about making the ideas of Adam Smith accessible to non-English reading Dutch people, a complete Dutch translation of *The Wealth of Nations* never came into being.

In his preface to the translation of Mrs. Marcet's *Conversations on Political Economy* Tydeman made reference to the favorable reception of this work by McCulloch and Malthus and also mentioned that since the publication of Verri's *Meditazioni sulla Economia Politica* in the Dutch language in 1801, economic literature in Holland had not been enriched by any translations of foreign works. Tydeman's translation of Mrs. Marcet's "Conversations" was motivated in part by his desire to test the receptivity of the Dutch people to this type of literature. His experience with this translation must have been sufficiently encouraging, so that he facilitated a translation of Senior's *Principles of Political Economy* in 1839, and a translation of a second work by Mrs. Marcet in 1840. In his preface to the translation of Senior's work, Tydeman expressed disagreement with Say's *Catechisme d'Économie Politique*, but he did not specify reasons explaining or supporting this statement.

Tydeman associated himself with a liberal approach to economic questions as it had been expressed by Jan Ackersdijck.

[20] H. W. Tydeman, Preface to *Grondbeginselen Der Staats-Huishoudkunde* by Mrs. Marcet (Dordrecht, 1825), p. xi.

In the preface to the translation of Senior's work, Tydeman advocated the establishment of free industry, free competition, and free economic development, and expressed agreement with Ackersdijck's position in regard to these questions. In a prize essay on the guilds, Tydeman condemned these institutions and defended free competition in his analysis.[21]

As far as is known, Tydeman never clarified explicitly why his interests in foreign economic literature were confined almost exclusively to writings of British origin. However, as has been noted, Tydeman was consistent in directing his attention toward British economists and in selecting English economic literature as a means for creating publicity for economics in Holland.

The first true Smithian economist in Holland was Jan Ackersdijck (1790–1861), who was one of the most outstanding teachers of economics in Holland during about thirty years of the first part of the nineteenth century. Ackersdijck considered it his foremost task to prepare a group of students for serious study of the field of economics. For this reason he emphasized his role as a teacher of economics above his role as a writer. Despite the smallness of the volume of Ackersdijck's writings and the narrow circumscription of these writings, his influence on nineteenth-century Dutch economics should not be underrated. Of Ackersdijck's students at least three achieved outstanding positions among Dutch economists, and it can be stated with certainty that Mees, Van Rees, Sloet Tot Oldhuis, Van Voorthuysen, and probably others were strongly influenced and inspired by Ackersdijck's teachings.

In view of Ackersdijck's influential role in the training of Dutch economists it is not without significance that he should have been so strongly oriented towards Smithian ideas. Unfortunately Ackersdijck never commented in detail or made any specific references to the ideas of Adam Smith or of other Dutch economists. Since Ackersdijck addressed himself to peculiarly Dutch economic problems in all his writings, information on his attitudes toward other economists or their theories is limited.

Ackersdijck held a commemorative speech on Adam Smith at the University of Utrecht in 1842. In this lecture, which was held

[21] H. W. Tydeman, *Verhandeling over de Vraag: Waren de inrigtingen der Gilden ...* Prijsvraag van het Zeeuwsch Genootschap (Middelburg, 1821).

in Latin but which was subsequently translated and printed in Dutch, a contrast was made between pre-Smithian and Smithian economics, with references to the economic ideas of Quesnay and the mercantilists as examples of pre-Smithian doctrines.[22] Adam Smith was thus portrayed as the founder of economics, and as the initial investigator of economics as a science. *The Wealth of Nations* was not described as a study in which all economic problems had been solved, and Ackersdijck admitted fully that Malthus, Ricardo, and Say had added considerably to the Smithian groundwork. The lecture also included discussion of primarily political obstacles which had for some sixty years barred widespread acceptance of Smith's ideas. However, noting a steady liberalization of economic policy in England as well as in other European countries, Ackersdijck hopefully envisioned the time when people would realize the extent of their indebtedness to the contributions of Adam Smith.

Van Rees has pointed out that Ackersdijck considered himself a follower of Malthus when he lectured to students about population theory.[23] Further information regarding Ackersdijck's evaluation of foreign economic literature is found in the previously mentioned correspondence between Jan Ackersdijck en Gijsbert Karel Van Hogendorp, during the years 1826–1828. These letters reveal that Ackersdijck had been highly impressed with the works of Ricardo and McCulloch. Ackersdijck accepted Ricardo's theory of value and of rent, together with his reasoning concerning the effects of protective tariffs, and endorsed Ricardo's and McCulloch's rejection of the corn laws. In addition it appeared to Ackersdijck that J. B. Say had introduced considerable obscurity into economics with his concept of "produits immatériels." Ackersdijck did not, however, think that capital could be appropriately reduced to terms of stored labor, along the lines suggested by Ricardo and McCulloch.[24]

Another part of the same correspondence was devoted to a discussion of Sismondi's *Nouveaux principes d'économie politique,*

[22] Jan Ackersdijck, "Adam Smith," *Tijdschrift voor Staathuishoudkunde en Statistiek*, II (1843), 1–18.

[23] Otto Van Rees, "De Wetenschappelijke Werkzaamheid van Mr. J. Ackersdijck," *Utrechtsche Studenten-Almanak* voor het jaar 1862, pp. 169–212.

[24] W. C. Mees, "Eene Briefwisseling Tusschen Gijsbert Karel Van Hogendorp En Prof. Jan Ackersdijck," *op. cit.*, pp. 111–116.

second edition (1827). Here again Ackersdijck supported Ricardo against Sismondi and Say, stating that Ricardo's basic principles were not erroneous but merely incomplete. Ricardo, said Ackersdijck, was by far the most logical thinker of the time. Besides, Ackersdijck took objection to the role of the state as delineated by Sismondi, since it was Ackersdijck's conviction that the usefulness of the state in economic life was correlated with its passivity. The state should refrain from intervention in all instances except when the maintenance of justice was required.[25]

Although the comments found in the above cited letters are very brief and hasty they must be regarded as extremely valuable and informative. Certainly it became clear in the correspondence that Adam Smith was not the sole foreign influence in Ackersdijck's orientation to economics. Apparently Ackersdijck had familiarized himself quite thoroughly with the works of British classical writers and was also well acquainted with writings of French economists. One is led to believe that Ackersdijck must have had solid reasons for assigning priority to British economists and for making a glorious speech about Adam Smith in 1842. However, the reasons for Ackersdijck's particular orientation towards foreign economics cannot be clearly established.

British economists further captured the interest of Otto Van Rees (1825–1868). Ackersdijck had singled out Van Rees as the most qualified person for the inheritance of his chair at the University of Utrecht. According to contemporaries of Van Rees, who commemorated him after his death, he had been a follower of Ackersdijck both as a teacher of economics at the University of Utrecht and as a strong adherent to Ackersdijck's economic ideas.[26]

Van Rees was one of the few nineteenth-century Dutch economists who did not become involved in writings of incidental nature. However, there are only few references to foreign economists in the writings of Van Rees, and therefore evidence is scarce on the extent to which Van Rees was swayed by foreign trends of economic thought. A few of Van Rees' comments are suggestive of his inclinations.

---

[25] *Ibid.*, pp. 120–122.
[26] Simon Vissering, "Mr. Otto Van Rees" in *Herinneringen*, III, 142–149; H. Toespraak, "Hulde Ter Nagedachtenis Van Mr. O. Van Rees," Gehouden in een Buitengewone Vergadering Der Vereeniging ter Bevordering Van Nuttige Kennis (1868); J. A. Fruin, "Levensbericht van Mr. Otto Van Rees," *op. cit.*, pp. 123–160.

In an inaugural speech at the University of Groningen, about the development of economic thought in Holland, Van Rees blamed such Dutch writers as Pestel, Luzac, and Kluit for advocating mercantillistic ideas even after the liberal thought of Verri and Smith had been introduced in Holland.[27] In a previously cited paper by Van Rees on Kluit the author had elaborated on Kluit's inconsistency regarding the acceptance of liberal views while at the same time unable to part with certain protectionistic ideas. Van Rees compared Kluit and Van Hogendorp and ranked Kluit as the less advanced of the two thinkers. In fact, Van Rees considered Van Hogendorp ahead of his time mainly because he was capable of understanding and appreciating fully the Smithian ideas, and because, contrary to Kluit, Van Hogendorp managed to disengage himself from the prejudices of his age. Nevertheless, Van Rees regretted that Van Hogendorp had not studied the British economists more thoroughly, saying that if he had paid more serious attention to such writers as Malthus and Ricardo, some of the flaws in his economic thinking could presumably have been avoided.[28] Van Rees also implied that Van Hogendorp might better have paid less attention to the works of J. B. Say and more to the British economists.[29]

W. C. Mees, a decidedly pre-eminent figure in the history of nineteenth-century Dutch economic thought, also subscribed to the pro-British disposition noted above. Though Mees cited economic literature only infrequently and though he rarely made reference to the views of economists, traces of Ricardian and Malthusian influence, and to a lesser extent of the influence of Adam Smith and John Stuart Mill can be found in his writings.

Mees reacted against the polemical nature of French economics, against the unwillingness of French economists to consider laws which had gloomy implications, and against their emphasis on "one-sided" industrial development, which according to Mees could not lead to progress unless accompanied by educational and moral advancement.[30] While Tydeman, Ackersdijck, and Van

[27] Otto Van Rees, *Redevoering Over De Staathuishoudkundige Geschiedenis Van Nederland* (Zutphen, 1858).

[28] Van Rees, on Van Hogendorp, *op. cit.*, ppl 198–200.

[29] *Ibid.*, p. 205.

[30] N. G. Pierson, "Levensbericht Van Mr. W. C. Mees," *op. cit.*, pp. 326–359; W. C. Mees, *Overzicht Van Eenige Hoofdstukken Der Staathuishoudkunde* (Amsterdam, 1866), Preface.

Rees had primarily criticized J. B. Say when discrediting French economic thought, Mees was more disturbed about the influence of Bastiat on economics.

Mees was probably the most forceful Dutch exponent of the Malthusian doctrine. In one of Mees' earlier publications on work houses for the poor, written in 1844, he stated that the entire study of poverty was directly related to population theory. Regarding population growth Mees was in complete agreement with Malthus. To him the Malthusian principles seemed "clear and simple," and he was surprised to find opposition to them.[31] In this publication as well as in one of his last works, "Overview Of Some Main Topics in Economics" (1866), he stated his basic conviction that improvement in the well being of a society was conditional upon moral restraint and improved education.[32]

Next to Malthus, Ricardian thought had exerted a considerable amount of influence on Mees' thinking. Pierson, in his article on Mees, has pointed to the strong reflection of Ricardian thought in Mees' "Overview." As a matter of fact, Pierson looked upon Ricardo's "Principles" and Mees' "Overview" as two rare gold-mines in the economic literature, and apparently considered them generally equivalent. But with respect to organizational skill, preciseness of reasoning, and logical rigor, Pierson found that Mees had surpassed his Britisch Master.[33]

In a paper on "Equal Distribution of Taxes" Mees made reference to the views of Adam Smith and John Stuart Mill on taxation. Though Mees considered Smith and Mill to be among the most outstanding economists he found that their writings on the subject of taxation were sources of great confusion. In Mees' opinion Smith had stated as one principle what in reality are two separate principles namely: (1) that taxes should be levied in proportion to respective abilities and (2) in proportion to respective benefits or protection enjoyed under the state. Mill, on the other hand, by rejecting the latter, which he identified as the quid pro quo principle, emphasized the former principle exclusively, that is, taxes should be levied in accordance with the

---

31 W. C. Mees, *De Werkinrichtingen Voor Armen Uit Een Staathuishoudkundig Oogpunt Beschouwd*, pp. 9–10.

32 W. C. Mees, *Overzicht Van Eenige Hoofdstukken Der Staathuishoudkunde.*

33 Pierson, "Levensbericht Van Mr. W. C. Mees," *op. cit.*, pp. 342–343.

means (abilities) of respective individuals, so that all shall make an equal sacrifice. Mees explained that the two principles have different implications and that both should be given consideration in the designing of fiscal policy. Smith had been responsible for confusion because he fused two separate rules into one; Mill had confused the issue with his downright rejection of one of the two equally significant principles.[34] For the purpose of this chapter only the following points are relevant: (1) that Mees regarded Adam Smith and John Stuart Mill as representative of the most outstanding economists and (2) that he regarded the views of Smith and Mill representative of ideas of economists on the subject of taxation, which probably influenced Mees in the development of his own approach to the subject of taxation.

Mees also made an "Attempt at Clarification of Some Concepts in Economics" in 1877, which exemplifies an approach to value theory very similar to that of Jevons and Menger. He referred to Jevons' *Theory of Political Economy* in this paper, but did not mention Menger's work, with which he apparently was not familiar. Mees did not consider himself in complete agreement with Jevons' utility theory, but his own concept of value, based on the relation of an individual to a good, stressed the subjective basis of value and was not strikingly different from the Jevonian concept. Thus Mees endorsed a trend of thought which was preparatory for the subsequent drift of Dutch economists towards the Austrian School of economics.[35]

The foreign influence on Dutch economists so far treated in this section has been exclusively British. Usually these writers had expressed unfavorable reactions to French economic thought. There were others among nineteenth-century Dutch economists who had also been susceptible to the influx of British economics. However, British influence on these figures was neither exclusive nor predominant, and for this reason they will be discussed as a separate group of economists.

We shall refer to Simon Vissering (1818–1888), J. L. De Bruyn

[34] Mees, "Opmerkingen Omtrent Gelijke Verdeeling Van Belasting," *op. cit.*, pp. 1–11.

[35] Mees, "Poging Tot Verduidelijking Van Eenige Begrippen In de Staathuishoud-kunde," *op. cit.*, Also see N. G. Pierson in *Verspreide Economische Geschriften*, II, 501–505, where he speaks of Mees as having anticipated the developments of marginal utility economics in England and Austria.

Kops (1822–1887), and B. W. A. E. Sloet Tot Oldhuis (1808–1884) as eclectic economists because they demonstrated allegiance to the ideas of French, British, and in some instances of German economists as well. Each of these economists paid considerable attention to French economic thought, and French economics made a dominant impression on each of these figures, at least during a certain part of his life. The Dutch economists to be discussed were receptive only to liberal French economic thought, and were usually hostile to French socialism.

It has been said of Vissering that during his training he was exposed primarily to French economic thought, but that subsequently he revised his own way of thinking after careful investigation of British economists.[36] Though the title of "Dutch Bastiat" given to Vissering may have been appropriate for certain phases of his thinking, it does not characterize his orientation towards foreign economics, later on in his life.[37]

Among the earliest writings of Vissering were a series of articles for a daily newspaper in 1845, in which he pleaded for repeal of the corn laws in Holland. In these articles, which were discussed in the previous chapter, Vissering referred to Adam Smith and Robert Peel as opponents of the corn laws, and cited similar views of Dutch economists as well. In 1846 Vissering published an article on "Robert Peel as a Statesman" in De Gids, and also translated and published a speech delivered by Robert Peel to the Lower House of Parliament in January 1846, on a "Proposed reform of the British Tariff."[38] As noted previously, Vissering in collaboration with D. A. Portielje wrote a "History of Tariff Reforms in England," in 1847, which was intended to influence the course of economic policy changes in Holland. These early writings clearly indicate Vissering's leaning towards liberal economic ideas in England, an orientation which he appears to have adopted at least partly on grounds of his policy objectives.

In 1848 Vissering published in De Gids a translation of an article by Michel Chevalier, titled "Question des Travailleurs"

---

[36] J. T. Buys, "Levensbericht van Mr. S. Vissering," Jaarboek Van De Koninklijke Akademie Van Wetenschappen (Amsterdam, 1889), p. 48.

[37] W. Van Der Vlught, "De Geestelijke Wetenschappen," in Historisch Gedenkboek, Eene Halve Eeuw, 1848–1898 (Amsterdam, 1898), p. 43.

[38] See De Gids (1846). Also Redevoering van Sir Robert Peel Over De Tariefshervorming (January 27, 1846), translated by S. Vissering (Amsterdam, 1846).

which had appeared in the *Revue des deux mondes* that same year. A controversy between Louis Blanc and Chevalier was continued in this article, revolving primarily around the "freedom to work" idea, apparently refuted by socialistic writers. Vissering attached a great deal of importance to "freedom to work," which is dealt with in a number of his writings.

Vissering, when appointed a chair at the University of Leiden in 1850, held an inaugural lecture on "Freedom as the Basic Principle of Economics." [39] He traced the meaning of freedom in the history of Western Society, up until the birth of liberal economics with the work of Adam Smith. According to Vissering the highest praise of Adam Smith was that expressed by a French historian: "Adam Smith a rehabilité le travail." At that time Vissering appreciated Adam Smith most because be regarded labor as the fundamental cornerstone of the economy, and because he looked upon freedom to work as the only lasting source of particular and general welfare. In the same lecture Vissering defined "freedom to work" as that freedom which assures to the individual the right to use his means and abilities in accordance with his own disposition. Vissering's "freedom to work" is equivalent to what is generally understood by free trade or laissez faire and, according to him, is intimately related to the doctrine of harmony, which Vissering presumably had inherited from Bastiat. [40]

Vissering early in his life resembled Bastiat in his expression of confidence in unconditional laissez faire and in his belief in the compatibility and complementarity of the interests of individual human beings. According to Vissering there were two basic principles of human behavior which were responsible for harmonious socio-economic action: (1) man pursues mainly selfish interests but at the same time (2) is dependent on the help of others. The counter-forces of these two principles are responsible for human cooperation. Vissering defined economics as "the science of economic life, which teaches, how, in accordance with natural laws, the particular dispositions of all individuals cooperate in the promotion of material well being and of the

[39] Simon Vissering, "Over Vrijheid, Het Grondbeginsel Der Staathuishoudkunde," in *Verzamelde Geschriften*, II (Leiden, 1889), 142–171.
[40] *Ibid.*, pp. 157–161. Also see Buys on Vissering, *op. cit.*, p. 52.

spiritual elevation of each individual and of all mankind." The objective of economics, he set forth, as "the resolution of the struggle between selfishness and neighborly love into beautiful harmony – freedom."[41]

During the next year Vissering discussed Bastiat's contributions in two separate articles; first in a paper on "Popular Economics" and later in an article entirely devoted to Bastiat.[42] Harmonism is not presented by Vissering as an original contribution of Bastiat, but Bastiat is described as having been the first to define harmony of individual interests as the foundation of the economic order.

A few years later, upon the occasion of a Dutch translation of McCulloch's *Essay on the Circumstances which Determine the Rate of Wages* (1826), Vissering, in an article on "Wages and Subsistence," expressed full agreement with McCulloch, one of the dominant exponents of the wage-fund doctrine.[43] Vissering especially emphasized the point that the lower limit of wages is determined by the basic needs of the worker. He deemed the low level of aspiration of Dutch laborers partly responsible for the low wage level in Holland. In his discussion of McCulloch's essay Vissering even admitted that the state had a certain obligation to promote the formation of capital in order to raise wages, and that the state also ought to raise the level of taste and aspiration of the population. He did not specify, however, how the state could achieve these tasks.

In the early 1860's Vissering's *Handboek Van Praktische Staathuishoudkunde* (Handbook of Practical Economics) appeared and this work yields further evidence of Vissering's growing admiration for British economists. On a number of subjects Vissering endorsed the views of Adam Smith. He found himself in agreement with Smith's definition of necessities and luxuries (as expressed in *The Wealth of Nations*) and in disagreement with Say's handling of the subject (in Traite d'Économie Politique). He agreed with Smith's opinion regarding the best sources of taxes and the best methods of tax collection, and endorsed his

---

[41] See Vissering's Inaugural lecture, *op. cit.*, pp. 153–159.
[42] Simon Vissering, "Populaire Staathuishoudkunde," *De Gids*, XV, Part I (1851), 19; Simon Vissering, "Frederic Bastiat," *De Gids*, XV, Part II (1851), 269–303.
[43] Simon Vissering, "Over Werkloonen en Volksvoeding," *op. cit.*, pp. 268–292.

view that the public debt should not be identified with national wealth.[44] In later editions of the "Handboek" references to Adam Smith became more frequent.

Vissering presented an elaborate treatment of the Malthusian population theory in the same work. In general he was sympathetic to the views of Malthus. However, he was optimistic about the relation between population and means of subsistence, since during the nineteenth century improved living standards had accompanied expanding populations in most European countries. It might be mentioned that in the 1878 edition of the *Handboek* a note was inserted to point out that Malthus' theory was again in vogue and that fear of overpopulation was one of the questions of the day.[45]

The *Handboek* also included a long discussion of the Ricardian theory of rent and of some of the criticisms raised against this theory. Though Vissering did not agree with the position which Bastiat and Carey had adopted in regard to Ricardo's theory of rent, he had his own reservations. Vissering criticized the following points: it is not necessarily true that the most fertile land is cultivated first; it is questionable whether land can be classified on the basis of the fertility as there are different types of fertility; technological advance, e.g., new fertilizers or new tools affect the fertility of land; and in fact prices of grain had not risen, in relation to the wage level, as the worker was able to purchase more grain with one day's wages in the nineteenth than in the seventeenth century.[46] Vissering credited Ricardo with having clarified why one plot of land yields a higher rent than another plot, either because it provided a larger supply of a commodity or a higher priced commodity or because it was more suitably located. Thus Vissering accepted Ricardo's differential rent, derived from location value or from a highly demanded output, while he disagreed with the diminishing returns aspect of the Ricardian rent theory.

Vissering also thought highly of John Stuart Mill. There are a

[44] Simon Vissering, *Handboek Van Praktische Staathuishoudkunde*, pp. 484–485 169, 175–176, 168–169, 277. All references to the *Handboek* are taken from the first, edition, though it was re-edited four times between 1860 and 1878.

[45] *Ibid.*, pp. 285–318. See *Handboek Van Praktische Staathoudkunde*, fourth edition, I (Amsterdam, 1878), 472.

[46] *Handboek*, pp. 542–547.

few references to Mill in the *Handboek*, which, however, are of no special significance. During 1867 and 1868 Vissering published a series of articles on higher education in *De Gids*, which were prefaced with a translation of J. S. Mill's ideas on the function of a university as expressed in an inaugural address at the University of St. Andrews in 1867. Mill's philosophy of higher education had made a strong impression on Vissering.[47]

It is quite apparent that when Vissering wrote his *Handboek*, his attitudes towards French economists in general, and towards Bastiat and Chevalier in particular, had become modified. As a matter of fact, he referred to Bastiat only when discussing the Ricardian theory of rent, and he did not accept Bastiat's criticism of this theory. J. B. Say was described by Vissering as a rather superficial economist, and Michel Chevalier was not mentioned at all.[48]

Vissering also expressed opposition to the German Historical School primarily because the historicists denied the existence of natural laws and because they overemphasized the role of the state in economic activities. Vissering looked upon German Historicism as an unsound outgrowth of a science to which the British economists had contributed the best, even if not the last words.[49] Thus Vissering was an eclectic of French and English economic doctrines, who was most susceptible to British economic thought during the latter part of his life.

In J. L. De Bruyn Kops French and British influences combined in a way so as to give a slightly different slant to his economic ideas than to those of Simon Vissering. Pierson had classified De Bruyn Kops as a follower of the French School of economists, though it seems that De Bruyn Kops was equally interested in the views of British economists. He was also favorably disposed to German Historicism. The fact that De Bruyn Kops was a more moderate laissez faire enthusiast than Vissering and De Bruyn Kops' attitude towards the Historical School mark the main distinction between the two Dutch economists.

It will be remembered that De Bruyn Kops was not essentially a teacher of economics. He had been a practicing lawyer, had

---

[47] Simon Vissering, "Studieën over Hooger Onderwijs," *Herinneringen*, III, 149–398.
[48] *Handboek*, p. 539.
[49] *Ibid.*, epilogue, pp. 407–414.

worked with the Department of Finance, had spent four years teaching at the Technical School of Delft and thirteen years as a member of the Second Chamber of the Dutch Parliament. Besides he had been founder and editor of *De Economist* from 1852 to 1887, and had writent the first home-grown economics textbook, *Beginselen Van Staathuishoudkunde* (Principles of Economics) published in 1850. Most of his ideas are found in his *Principles* and in the numerous articles published in *De Economist*.

De Bruyn Kops' writings were devoted primarily to the diffusion and popularization of economics among the entire population. This objective was explicitly stated in his preface to the *Principles* as well as in the subtitle of *De Economist*: "Journal for all classes, for the promotion of national well being by means of the diffusion of elementary principles." Primarily he intended to familiarize his readers with the factors involved in practical economic issues, which he felt every citizen with political responsibility ought to understand. One does not find lengthy discussions of theoretical issues, of controversies between economists, or of the development of different concepts in his *Principles*, nor does one find references to or citations of the classical economists. Throughout the book theories, concepts, and solutions to practical questions are usually presented as though they were firmly and generally accepted and elements of doubt are carefully concealed. Yet, this elementary didacticism, though it characterized De Bruyn Kops' *Principles*, was not characteristic of his general attitude toward economics.[50] De Bruyn Kops was far from endorsing the opinion that economics largely embodied irrefutable truths. In fact, he made it a point to express caution against doctrinairism and scientific orthodoxy.[51]

With a number of contemporary economists De Bruyn Kops shared the conviction that the wealth of a nation and the functioning of an economy were determined by immutable natural laws. Despite his belief in the perseverance of basic natural laws, De Bruyn Kops admitted that interpretations of the laws depended on concrete data and that the solutions to concrete

[50] See P. Hennipman, "J. L. De Bruyn Kops," *De Economist*, C (1952), 785–815.
[51] See preface to fifth edition to *Beginselen Van Staathuishoudkunde* (1873), pp. xi–xii.

problems could differ under changing circumstances.[52] Thus De Bruyn Kops indicated his awareness of historical, relativistic elements in economic phenomena. Furthermore, he accepted the doctrine of harmony of interests though he never cited the source of this particular influence. That the pursuit of individual self-interest could be relied upon to achieve socially satisfactory results was in his opinion one of the most important truths brought to light by policital economy.[53]

Originally, De Bruyn Kops had accepted Say's definition of economic goods, which included both material and non-material objects, discussing it in connection with the distinction between productive and unproductive labor. In the fifth edition of his *Principles* De Bruyn Kops no longer found the two above distinctions feasible or useful, because material and non-material goods as well as physical and non-physical labor were in many cases intimately fused, and therefore inseparable, even for analytical purposes.[54] He therefore recommended that all efforts which directly and indirectly contributed to the general wealth should be regarded as productive labor. Yet, in the course of his discussion, De Bruyn Kops compared the services of the teacher with those of the barber and found only the former productive; the latter in his opinion did not contribute to national wealth. De Bruyn Kops included in his concept of wealth all goods which were both useful and exchangeable. Value, he explained, originates in society and can only exist where people exchange goods. For a man in isolation goods have more or less utility, but no value. Wealth is composed of goods which are useful and scarce, and therefore, have exchange value.[55]

The kernel of all of De Bruyn Kops' writings is to be found

---

[52] *Ibid.*, p. x–xiii.

[53] J. L. De Bruyn Kops, *Beginselen Van Staathuishoudkunde*, fifth edition ('S Gravenhage, 1873), pp. 479–485.

[54] *Ibid.*, pp. 201–202.

[55] *Ibid.*, pp. 201–213; on value see pp. 8–18. Pierson, who criticized Say in a number of different writings, reviewed De Bruyn Kops' *Principles* (third edition) unfavorably, primarily because of the author's support of Say's views. More recently Hennipman has pointed to the dubious aspect of classifying De Bruyn Kops as a product of the French School. Hennipman doubted that De Bruyn Kops would have considered himself a follower of the French School exclusively. See N. G. Pierson's review of *Beginselen Van Staathuishoudkunde*, third edition, in *Verspreide Economische Geschriften*, I, 390–412. P. Hennipman, "J. L. De Bruyn Kops," *op. cit.*, pp. 803–805.

in his vindication of liberal economics. De Bruyn Kops wanted all obstacles to a freely functioning economy removed and interferences with the economic liberties of individuals done away with. Phrases as "freedom of exchange" and "freedom of industry" are frequently encountered in his writings. The idea of "freedom to work," as Vissering had used it, was employed by De Bruyn Kops almost as a slogan. He designated this phrase to encompass economic freedom in general; more specifically it referred to the freedom of an individual to accept the kind of employment he chooses, to produce as he pleases, as much as he pleases, and to dispose of his output as he wishes.[56] The economy was deemed to function most effectively when governmental interference was at its minimum.

De Bruyn Kops considered Bastiat inferior by far to Chevalier, in his grasp of fundamental principles as well as in respect to his practical insights. His admiration for Chevalier was expressed in an article published in De Economist, which included a translation of the inaugural lecture delivered by Chevalier on the occasion of his resuming the chair at the College De France in 1866, and in an obituary of Chevalier also published in De Economist.[57] Chevalier's inaugural lecture dealt primarily with the principle of "freedom to work" which allegedly comprised all economic liberties, and a principle which De Bruyn Kops advocated in many of his writings. In several articles on the state of economics in general De Bruyn Kops also acknowledged contributions of such French economists as J. B. Say, Dunoyer, Passy, Courcelle-Seneuil, Garnier, and Rossi.[58]

In the same articles De Bruyn Kops' appraisals of certain British economists were marked by an equally favorable tone. Adam Smith was recognized as the founder of economics and the initiator of the British School. On the whole, De Bruyn Kops neglected the contributions of Ricardo while he discussed certain ideas of Smith, Malthus, and Mill on various occasions. In his *Principles* the subject of rent was ignored altogether. In his

---

[56] J. L. De Bruyn Kops, *Beginselen Van Staathuishoudkunde*, fifth edition, p. 219. Also see *De Economist*, XIV (1865), 11.

[57] J. L. De Bruyn Kops, "De Vooruitgang Der Staathuishoudkunde," *De Economist*, XVI (1867), 1–22, and "Michel Chevalier," *De Economist*, XXIX (1880), Part I, 65–75.

[58] *De Economist*, XI (1862), 1–16; XIV (1865), 1–20; XIX (1880), Part 1, 65–75.

discussion of the population problem De Bruyn Kops referred to Malthus' "Essay." The population problem was always related to poverty by De Bruyn Kops, and the subject of poverty consti-tuted what he considered one of the most important chapters of his *Principles*. De Bruyn Kops appreciated Malthus for having clarified fundamental issues relating to the problem of destitution and considered the Malthusian population theory responsible for policy improvements in regard to pauperism. It will be re-membered from the previous chapter, in which De Bruyn Kops' views on population and pauperism have been dealt with, that he argued for state intervention on behalf of the poor, as he con-sidered the problem of pauperism outside the realm of production and exchange. He found support for his position in John Stuart Mill whom he referred to as "the leading economist of the present time."[59]

It has been mentioned above that De Bruyn Kops was a more circumscribed free trader than Vissering. He regarded state intervention in certain areas of the economy as necessary and fruitful, when Vissering argued for a "hands off" policy. It should be noted also that De Bruyn Kops' attitude to the German Historicists and Socialists of the Chair was a favorable one as he considered this movement a healthy reaction to the extreme position developed by the Manchester School and by such French economists as Bastiat[60] De Bruyn Kops doubted whether the new approach developed by the Historical School would actually replace "the old economics" but if the new movement would serve merely to convince economists that laissez faire was not to be interpreted as a "dolce far niente," then it would have per-formed a most useful function. A hybridized French-British intellectual heritage was at least partly responsible for the liberal economic views of De Bruyn Kops, but did not arouse in him an antipathy for the German Historical School.

B. W. A. E. Sloet Tot Oldhuis, the last member of this group, can be discussed rather briefly. His writings were limited to articles and reviews in the journal he founded: *Tijdschrift voor*

---

[59] See *De Economist*, XI (1862), 15. Also J. L. De Bruyn Kops, *Over het Beginsel van Armenverzorging door den Staat (Leiden–Amsterdam*, 1852), p. 24.

[60] J. L. De Bruyn Kops, *Beginselen Van Staathuishoudkunde*, preface to fifth edition, p. xi; also "Aan Den Lezer," in *De Economist*, XXV (1876), Part I.

Staathuishoudkunde en Statistiek 1841–1875, and to prefaces of two translations which carried his name: *Économie politique, ou Principes de la science des richesse* by Joseph Droz and *Théorie des peines et des récompenses* by Jeremy Bentham. Despite the fact that Sloet Tot Oldhuis was also a student of Jan Ackersdijck, the first Dutch Smithian economist, he appears to have drifted more in the French than in the British direction. Sloet Tot Oldhuis also indicated some interest in German economic thought.

Sloet Tot Oldhuis described Droz' *Économie politique, ou Principes de la science des richesse* as one of the clearest and most concise introductory books in economics, highly suited for the popularization of economics among the Dutch public. Since Holland had become a representative democracy in 1848, Sloet Tot Oldhuis considered it of utmost importance that the average citizen have an understanding of basic economic issues and be familiar with the common misconceptions in economics. He recommended Droz' book particularly to the teachers of elementary schools as he was strongly in favor of introducing the teaching of economics on the elementary level of education. The translation of Droz' book received a second edition in 1850. In his preface to the Dutch edition of Dumont's version of Bentham's work, noted above, Sloet Tot Oldhuis did not reveal the motivation for translating this particular book into the Dutch language.

In his journal Sloet Tot Oldhuis discussed most of the books, articles, journals, dissertations, and translations of foreign books which appeared in the field of economics. He also published in this quarterly a sequence of articles on "The Main Trends in Economics" (Grondtrekken Der Staathuishoudkunde), in which he compared and contrasted the views of foreign and Dutch economists on a variety of subjects. His many reviews as well as his articles portray Sloet Tot Oldhuis as widely read in the field of economics but as only superficially acquainted with economic literature. Rarely did he penetrate the surface of any subject; hardly ever did he clarify his own views towards a particular problem or towards a work he was reviewing. Sloet Tot Oldhuis belonged to the liberal economists of his time and opposed all socialistic and communistic movements. Within the framework of his orientation, the most outstanding feature of Sloet Tot

Oldhuis as an economist was a lack of definite viewpoints and opinions along with a lack of discriminating judgment.

One finds that in Sloet Tot Oldhuis' journal the ideas of British, French, and German economists are almost equally well represented. He was interested in the development of economic literature, the development of economic ideas, and the teaching of economics in an increasing number of educational institutions. Thus he recognized all signs of interest in the field, encouraged all steps toward new channels of investigation, and rewarded all efforts at clarification of economic phenomena and spreading of economic knowledge.[61] With similar enthusiasm he spoke of works by J. B. Say, Miss Martineau, Bastiat, De Bruyn Kops, Roscher, Richard Whately, W. C. Mees, Mrs. Marcet, K. H. Rau and others. It is surprising that anyone could have pronounced evaluations so alike on such diverse performances in the study of economics. In his articles on "The Main Trends in Economics" published in the first twelve volumes of his journal between 1841 and 1855, Sloet Tot Oldhuis paid tribute to the views of Say, Droz, Storch, Garnier, Chevalier, Rossi, Blanqui, and Martineau; to the views of Smith, Ricardo, Malthus, and McCulloch as well as to Von Schloezer, Rau, Von Jacob, Soden, Roscher, and Kraus. Say rather than Smith was regarded as the founder of the study of economics and was cited more frequently than any other writer.[62] Although it was never stated explicitly, Sloet Tot Oldhuis follow- ed J. B. Say to a large extent in his thinking about economic problems.

In the late 1850's the foreign impact on Dutch economics stimulated some interest in investigations on value theory which ought to be noted here. In 1858 and 1859 two studies were sub- mitted in response to a prize question suggested by Vissering at the University of Leiden. T. M. C. Asser received a gold medal for his "Study of the economic concept of Value" and S. Van Houten received a silver medal, or second prize, for his "Study on Value."[63] In both studies the development of subjective value

[61] Sloet Tot Oldhuis showed particular admiration for Richard Whately for having introduced the teaching of economics into 4000 elementary schools in Great Britain, *Tijdschrift voor Staathuishoudkunde en Statistiek*, VIII (1852), 473, and IX (1853), 111.

[62] B. W. A. E. Sloet Tot Oldhuis, "Grondtrekken Der Staathuishoudkunde," *Tijdschrift voor Staathuishoudkunde en Statistiek*, II (1844), Part II, 413.

[63] T. M. C. Asser, *Verhandeling Over Het Staathuishoudkundig Begrip Der Waarde* (Amsterdam, 1858); S. Van Houten, *Verhandeling Over De Waarde* (Groningen, 1859).

theory was emphasized. Whereas Asser was very much influenced by concepts of value as developed by Storch, Senior and Bastiat, Van Houten was a follower mainly of Whately, MacLeod, and Courcelle-Seneuil. The studies are mentioned primarily because they reflect an interest in value theory, a subject which had not been considered previously in the Dutch economic literature.[64] Furthermore, it is interesting to note the emphasis on subjective value by both authors, in view of the fact that about fifteen years later the Dutch tended to drift primarily in the Austrian direction.

SOME GENERALIZATIONS ABOUT THE FOREIGN IMPACT ON DUTCH ECONOMIC THOUGHT

Dutch economists during the nineteenth century showed a great deal of interest in the development of liberal economic ideas in foreign countries. In the late eighteenth and early nineteenth centuries the views of German cameralists gained some popularity in Holland. Thereafter liberal economics of the English and French variety exerted major influence on the development of Dutch economic thought. Generally speaking, Dutch economists expressed opposition to protectionism, socialism, and communism as well as to German Historicism. This is not to say that socialism and German Historicism found no spokesmen whatsoever in Holland. However, at least until the 1870's, such advocates remained largely outside the mainstream of Dutch economic thought.

Dutch liberal economists were divided into two groups for the purposes of this chapter. One group was centered around Jan Ackersdijck and consisted of economists with a predominantly

---

[64] It was pointed out in the previous chapter that nineteenth-century Dutch economists largely concentrated on applied economics. The above mentioned studies on value theory as well as a number of dissertations indicate a tendency of Dutch economists to become involved with investigations of theoretical nature. Vissering sponsored a number of dissertations of this type though he himself incorporated little theoretical analysis into his writings. J. D'Aulnis De Bourouill, *Het Inkomen De Maatschappij* (Leiden, 1874); J. F. B. Baert, *Adam Smith En Zijn Onderzoek Naar Den Rijkdom Der Volkeren* (Leiden, 1858); Thomas Van Stok, *De Stelsels der Staathuishoudkundigen Omtrent Grondrente Ontvouwd en Beoordeeld* (Rotterdam, 1858), are cases in point. The works mentioned are among the first investigations by Dutch economists which were not directly related to practical economic problems.

British orientation. The second group of economists displayed eclectic tendencies and manifested combined interests in British, French, and in some instances in German economic thought. Symptomatic of most of the economists under consideration was the lack of explicit agreement or identification with individual foreign economists or foreign schools. They rarely analyzed the approach or total contribution of predecessors. Most references to foreign economists were made in the context of specific issues. For this reason the analysis of foreign influences in the Dutch literature had to be based on selected comments on, citations of, and references to foreign economists as well as on the translations of speeches, essays, and books of these economists.

Although it was characteristic of Dutch economists to address themselves to practical questions primarily, it might be pointed out that the followers of British thought generally showed greater inclination towards theory than the more eclectic economists. Although all the writings of Ackersdijck were of incidental nature, his correspondence with Van Hogendorp revealed his preoccupation with and serious interest in theoretical concepts. His student W. C. Mees and Mees' disciple N. G. Pierson, were the most outstanding Dutch economists of the nineteenth century. On the other hand, economists interested in British, French, and German writers tended to be less theoretically oriented. This was true of Vissering as well as of De Bruyn Kops and Sloet Tot Oldhuis. The last two were more elementary in their writings than Vissering, but even Vissering did not devote much attention to economic theory. The contrast is clearly brought out in a comparison of Vissering's writings to those of W. C. Mees. It is also evident that Ricardo influenced the followers of British thought (Ackersdijck and Mees) while the eclectic economists tended to ignore Ricardo's doctrines. On the whole very little, if any, opposition is found to Smith or Malthus, and considerable approval was expressed for McCulloch and John Stuart Mill.

While the writings of British economists were frequently consulted on questions of trade policy, taxation, and wages, it appears that the French literature was often referred to in the context of resistance to socialism. At least this is one possible way of explaining the emphasis placed on Chevalier and Bastiat, especially in view of the fact that all the short, anti-socialistic writings of

Bastiat were translated into Dutch. It is also reasonable to suppose that interest in the liberal French literature was motivated by the pursuit of popularization in economics. Apparently Dutch economists were acutely aware of their task as popularizers so that scholars as Van Rees and Mees lectured to the public on questions economic in nature and men like Vissering, De Bruyn Kops, and Sloet Tot Oldhuis directed their literary efforts to a lay audience most of the time. Most of the economists here considered conceived of their educational function as extending beyond the university, and this in a way channeled their interests in foreign literature. Especially the foreign literature chosen for Dutch translation appears to have been selected with the popularization objective in mind, and it seems that a number of French economic writings were particularly suited for popularizing. At least this aspect was often mentioned in the prefaces of translations.

From the list of economic writings translated into Dutch, which constitutes Appendix A of this study, it will be observed that a number of French writings translated around the 1850's were textbook material. The need for elementary and textbook type of books was derived from the popularization motive and the expressed desire to introduce economics into the curriculum of high schools and elementary schools. This serves to explain in part why Adam Smith, David Ricardo and Malthus were never translated into Dutch, while Bastiat, Baudrillart, Blanqui, Droz, Garnier, De Hamal, Martineau and Say were published in Dutch editions, as were Mrs. Marcet, Richard Whately, one work by McCulloch. and surprisingly, John Stuart Mill's *Principles* in 1875.

Early phases of Dutch interest in German liberal economists had been noticed in Tydeman, in the Dutch writers on value theory after the middle of the century, and in Sloet Tot Oldhuis. Eventually a liberal economist, De Bruyn Kops, welcomed German Historicism though the movement as such never gained much influence in Holland. On the whole the German impact on Dutch economic thought during most of the nineteenth century was overshadowed by British and French influence.

Studies on theoretical topics during the late 1850's and some of the writings of W. C. Mees served as preparatory steps to the subsequent reception of Austrian economics in Holland during the 1870's. In 1874 a dissertation was written under Vissering on the marginal economics of Jevons.[65] As a matter of fact, the Dutch author, D'Aulnis De Bourouill, claimed responsibility for the initial contact between Jevons and Walras. Despite the fact that Jevons and Walras were known to the Dutch, the Austrian School had a predominant impact on late nineteenth-century economic thought in Holland. Thus the liberal tradition in economics was reinforced by a new current, and continued on as a fusion of foreign doctrines rather than as an autonomous movement of ideas.

---

[65] J. D'Aulnis De Bourouill, *Het Inkomen Der Maatschappij* (Leiden, 1874). See preface on correspondence of D'Aulnis De Bourouill with Jevons and Walras.

CHAPTER VIII

SUMMARY AND INTERPRETATION

In the course of the nineteenth century economics gradually acquired the status of an independent branch of investigation and knowledge in Holland. Our main concern in this study has been with this change in the status of economics both as a professional field and as a discipline, for Dutch economists made no contributions to speak of to economic thought or analysis. Various factors played a part in bringing about this change in the status of economics in Holland. The roles of these factors have been explored in detail in earlier chapters. In the present chapter an attempt will be made to combine the various fragments of this study into a total picture. Discussion will be centered around the following points: the conflict between law and economics; the status of academic economics versus that of economics as a profession; the policy-orientedness of Dutch economics; the emphasis of Dutch economists on popularization; and the effect of the cleavage between economics and law upon conceptions of the role of theory. It is taken for granted, of course, that those institutional, educational, and professional arrangements which helped to determine the status of economics in nineteenth-century Dutch university and professional circles, also had bearing on the nature and quality of economic inquiry carried on in Holland.

THE CONFLICT BETWEEN LAW AND ECONOMICS

During all of the nineteenth century, responsibility for providing training in economics was vested in the law faculties of Dutch universities. This meant that economics was merely a subject auxiliary to law, that there was no training program for economists per se, and that economics was always taught by a person of legal training and background. During most of the nineteenth century Dutch law faculties consisted of no more than two to three professors. One of these law-faculty members was assigned the task of teaching economics and statistics in addition to responsibility for several law courses. Usually Dutch law faculties offered only a single economics course, in which the entire field was to be covered. In short, only a fraction of one professor's time was allocated to the teaching of the single course of economics offered.

Provision for training in economics and statistics represented only an insignificant portion of the total law curriculum, with the result that opportunities for a law student to develop his interests in economics during the period of his formal education were extremely limited. Under the given circumstances it should not have come as a surprise that only few of the law students indicated an interest in economics beyond the passing of required examinations. Lawyers, after all, are trained primarily in the practice of casuistry and in the application of rules to individual cases. Inasmuch as economics is concerned with the empirical study of certain aspects of human behavior, if differs from law in scope, in objectives, and in methods of analysis. The location of academic economics in the Dutch law faculties thus hindered the advancement of the discipline, since economics was subjected to and combined with a field of study of which the overall objectives, the practical purposes, and the techniques of reasoning were markedly different.

The academic framework in which economics was offered shaped both the type of training to which nineteenth-century Dutch economists were exposed as students, and the environment in which they functioned after they became teachers of economics. The single economics course provided for in the law faculties did not allow for much differentiation of economics into separate fields. From the limited information that is available about the manner in which economics was taught in Holland during the nineteenth century it seems that strong emphasis was placed upon practical issues and upon the discussion of specifically

Dutch economic problems. Stress upon applied economics characterized the economics courses offered by Ackersdijck, Van Rees,
and Vissering, it is reported. Given the above academic and
teaching context, it is unlikely that representative economics
professors had the time or opportunity in nineteenth-century
Holland to devote themselves to much theoretical inquiry or to
fundamental empirical investigation.

In view of the position of economics in the university system
one might expect the writings of economists in the law faculties
to differ from the writings of those employed outside the academic sphere. It is difficult, however, to discover such differences
(if they existed) because of the smallness of the number of Dutch
economists who were outstanding authors in the nineteenth
century. The group of representative economists considered in
this study included only three figures with non-academic careers.
Of these three, De Bruyn Kops and Sloet Tot Oldhuis held
political offices for considerable parts of their lives, and the
available information does not indicate that their ideas and
modes of reasoning differed notably from those characteristic of
their academic colleagues. The third member of this group,
W. C. Mees, who was employed in an executive capacity with
the Netherlands Bank for the major part of his life, gave evidence
of a stronger interest in theoretical questions and in theoretical
analysis than did any of his contemporaries. Nevertheless, it is
not possible to determine what Mees' interests would have been
had he remained in the academic, law-faculty environment.[1]
Even so, although the available information does not permit
extensive comparison of the work of economists in law faculties
with that of economists in non-academic situations, it needs to
be remembered that the only figure who, between 1800 and 1870,
directed a part of his efforts to the study of economic theory,
namely W. C. Mees, never held a chair at a law faculty.

---

[1] It is of interest to note here that H. P. G. Quack resigned his position at the law
faculty of the University of Utrecht for the post of Secretary of the Netherlands Bank
in 1877, and explained that the latter employment was chosen because he expected
that it would enable him to work on a book which he was then planning. H. P. G.
Quack, *Herinneringen*, Tweede Druk (Amsterdam, 1915), pp. 239-249.

STATUS OF ACADEMIC ECONOMICS VERSUS THAT
OF ECONOMICS AS A PROFESSION

During the nineteenth century the academical and professional status of economics underwent uneven change. The course of change in the status of economics in the realm of education may be examined first. Responsibility for the provision of courses in economics remained under control of Dutch law faculties until the early twentieth century. However, certain changes introduced in the Dutch system of higher education during the second half of the nineteenth century made the university situation more favorable to the development of economics in Holland than it had been earlier in the century. Of these changes two stand out: (1) the discontinuation of Latin as the official university language, and (2) the departure from the four-faculty structure of universities.

The use of Latin had early been held as an obstacle to the development of economics, since this language, because it lacked words and concepts appropriate for the verbalizing of economic subject matter, made progress in economic thought and writing quite difficult. Hence liberalization of the Latin requirement in the 1840's and 1850's, in respect to economic dissertations and inaugural speeches, was welcomed both by Dutch economists and by students of economics. The rigid four-faculty structure was altered in the 1870's when provisions were made for the establishment of an independent faculty of natural sciences at Dutch universities. This change, although it did not immediately affect the actual status of economics in universities, made the prospect for eventually setting up a separate faculty of economics appear more hopeful. It so happened, however, that the ties binding economics to Dutch law faculties did not begin to be severed until 1913, when the Rotterdam School of Economics was founded. Not until 1922, however, was a separate faculty of economics, generally referred to as the sixth faculty of Dutch universities, set up at the University of Amsterdam.

It should be noted, furthermore, that the general stress on vocational and professional training in Holland affected the development of economics as an independent field of knowledge within the educational system. That concern was expressed at various times during the nineteenth century for the lack of training programs in Holland for careers in business and industry, has been noted in Chapter IV. The Dutch became aware of this lack when business-education programs established in foreign countries began to attract the Dutch students. It should be remembered also that the first Dutch chair of economics, which was not within a law faculty, was founded at the Technical School of Delft (a school existing primarily for the training of engineers), in 1906. Furthermore, it must be recalled that the Rotterdam School of Economics was first set up in 1913 to offer a two-year training program suited to prepare students for business positions, employment with chambers of commerce and trade unions, for diplomatic services, and for services as accountants. The school came into existence primarily as a result of incentive and financial support originating in private business circles, and the curriculum at first emphasized a vocational training program. The sixth faculty at the University of Amsterdam also had a pronounced business-school orientation when it was first founded. Realization of the need for vocational training rather than activity by or on the part of academic economists thus gave momentum to the movement to emancipate economics from a situation of subordinacy in Dutch law faculties.

Improvement in the opportunities open to economists qua economists – that is, in the professional status of the economist – made for progress in Dutch economics much as did the changes occurring in the occupational situation and in the educational arrangements of Holland. During the early part of the nineteenth century the professional opportunities open to Dutch economists, trained primarily to be lawyers, were limited to the pursuit of careers in the field of law or to engagements as teachers in the field of law and economics. Towards the middle of the century, the variety of professional services which economists were called upon to provide began to increase. Dutch economists began to be employed by government agencies and commissions, by chambers of commerce, by the central bank, and by newspapers and journals. They were also called upon to set up statistical organizations, to participate in debates, and to hold political offices. In part as a result of the enlargement of public interest in their skills Dutch economists began to found economic journals and to establish economic societies such as the *Maatschappij Felix Meritis*. In short, economics began significantly to undergo professionalization during the second half of the nineteenth century, and economists came to be recognized as professional people and to be called upon in their professional capacities instead of merely as lawyers. Furthermore, professional selfconsciousness developed among Dutch economists in some measure, and this was particularly expressed in their establishment of organs of communication, such as economic journals and economic societies intended to serve the professional interests and needs of economists.

However, inasmuch as the recognition of economics as a profession preceded its recognition as an independent discipline in the academic world, academic economists were diverted from developing professional self-consciousness within the university environment. Dutch academic economists during the nineteenth century apparently identified themselves with the lawyers who were their colleagues in the law faculties. There is no evidence that Dutch economics professors were disturbed about the subordinate position of economics in the law faculties or that they were interested in the setting up of independent faculties of economics at Dutch universities. If such thoughts ever entered the minds of Dutch economists they were apparently not stated explicitly, and one has to assume that economists were apathetic in respect to this matter. According to the available information, academic economists played only a minimal role in the establishment of the Rotterdam School of Economics and of the economics faculty at the University of Amsterdam.

THE POLICY-ORIENTEDNESS OF DUTCH ECONOMICS

The fact that economics in nineteenth-century Holland was expanding primarily in the professional sphere sheds some light on the predominantly applied character and policy-orientedness of Dutch economics. Reference has been made previously to the heavy emphasis put on applied economics by teachers of the subject in Dutch law faculties. Possibly the economics courses were designed to concentrate on practical questions because this made more sense in the training of law students than would discussion of theoretical and conceptual problems. Heavy concentration on practical economic issues was disclosed also by the review of the major writings of the representative group of Dutch economists presented in earlier chapters. The nature of the economics offered in the Dutch classroom thus resembled closely that of Dutch economic literature.

The majority of the writings of representative Dutch economists were policy-oriented. They concentrated particularly on a few fields: population and poverty, trade policy, currency and banking issues, and public finance. Nineteenth-century Dutch economic literature thus reflected to a large extent the economic problems faced by the Dutch economy during this century. In a sense an outstanding characteristic of seventeenth- and eighteenth-century Dutch economic writings was present in nineteenth-century Dutch economic literature; in each period much of what was written was largely incidental in character.

A few, exceptional Dutch economists produced work that was not immediately practical in nature. W. C. Mees was mentioned earlier as having published a book on value, price, and distribution theory, namely his "Overview of some Main Topics in Economics." On the whole his writings were wider in scope and more general in character than were those of most of his contemporaries. Another exceptional figure was Otto Van Rees, who avoided exclusive involvement with the immediately practical by concentrating on economic history and the history of economic thought. In his own way Van Rees was as unique among nineteenth-century Dutch economists as was W. C. Mees. Further examples of writings which were not on problems then facing the Dutch economy were two studies on value theory published in the late 1850's by T. M. C. Asser and S. Van Houten. These works, though they were primarily discussions of the treatment of value theory by different foreign economists, represent the first attempts of Dutch economists to deal with value theory. Both authors strongly emphasized the subjective approach to value theory. Among the home-grown textbooks for economics there were those of De Bruyn Kops and Vissering, both of which went through several editions. A number of additional textbooks were translated from foreign languages.

One might still ask why nineteenth-century Dutch economists put such heavy emphasis on applied economics. Demands of the political offices held by many Dutch economists, together with the variety of services of a practical nature that these economists were called upon to contribute, must have given a practical turn to their minds. Furthermore, it is possible that the energies of Dutch academic economists were absorbed to a large extent by concrete problems which had to be solved within the Dutch economy. Economists seem to have been less numerous in Holland at the time than problems in need of solutions revealed to be necessary. It has been pointed out, furthermore, that the academic economist serving the Dutch law faculties, was burdened with a teaching load that was heavy as well as diversified, and it is possible therefore that the representative academic economist was unable, for sheer lack of time, to devote himself to theoretical and historical questions. One may also venture the guess that in the given cultural-educational context a contribution to the solution of practical questions tended to be more highly rewarded than was a scholarly investigation of scientific questions. For this reason Dutch economists may have been more challenged by questions of applied economics, with the result that they were swayed in the direction of an all too exclusive concentration on matters of economic policy.

THE EMPHASIS
OF DUTCH ECONOMISTS ON POPULARIZATION

Dutch economists may be divided into two groups in respect of their reasons for advocating the popularization of economics. Otto Van Rees, W. C. Mees, and De Bruyn Kops, for example, subscribed to the idea that educational and intellectual advancement of the population at large would lead to economic progress. First of all they believed that an extension of education in general would serve to raise the level of morality in any society and thus would help it to cope with problems of laziness, overindulgence in drinking, and wastefulness. Furthermore, they felt that educational advancement would provide solutions to such problems as poverty, unemployment, and overpopulation; it would also enhance the savings potential of a society which was considered essential for economic betterment. Vissering and Sloet Tot Oldhuis, on the other hand, based their interest in popular education on the responsibilities related to general suffrage.

The two types of approaches made to the popularization of economics will be discussed separately. Van Rees, for example, founded a journal called *Pantheon* for the purpose of spreading useful knowledge and for advancing education among the lower classes. Van Rees also contributed to an adult education program by holding evening lectures. W. C. Mees gave evening lectures on economics in Rotterdam during a short period of his life, and emphasized the importance of educational advancement for economic progress in a number of his writings. De Bruyn Kops founded his journal *De Economist* as "a journal for all classes" which he dedicated to "the promotion of national welfare by means of propagation of elementary principles." His main objective was to provide useful knowledge to the public at large. In the preface to his book on *Principles* De Bruyn Kops stated explicitly that he had attempted to make his subject comprehensible to all, and apologized to the more advanced reader in case the book seemed too elementary and the illustrations overly simple.[2] Although De Bruyn Kops did not feel that economics should be taught in elementary schools, he looked forward to its introduction into secondary and professional schools.[3] Even though Mees was probably as dedicated as were Van Rees and De Bruyn Kops to the facilitation of educational opportunities to all classes of the Dutch population, he did not address himself to the lay reader in his economic writings. De Bruyn Kops, on the other hand, made a deliberate attempt in practically all his writings to communicate to a wide and partly uneducated audience. Van Rees managed to write on both the scholarly and the popular level, depending on the nature of the subject matter and the object he had in mind.

Simon Vissering and Sloet Tot Oldhuis emphasized the importance of popular education primarily because they insisted

---

[2] J. L. De Bruyn Kops, *Beginselen Van Staathuishoudkunde*, fifth edition, see Preface.

[3] J. L. De Bruyn Kops, "Het Onderwijs In De Staathuishoudkunde," *De Economist*, VI (1857), 129–142, especially p. 137, and "Eenige Gedachten Over De Economische Wetenschap," *De Economist*, XI (1862), 1–17, especially pp. 15–16.

that the success of a democratic government rested on the enlightenment of the population. These economists became increasingly aware that their function as educators had to extend to the public at large, that economic enlightenment was one of the prerequisites of meaningful suffrage, and was also essential for the prevention of socialism. The literary efforts of Vissering and Sloet Tot Oldhuis were influenced accordingly.

During the earlier part of his career Vissering had intentions of writing an elementary manual of economics which was never completed. However, a piece that was to serve as introduction to the manual "Money and Economic Exchanges," was written in 1856. Another essay on money, written in popular style and called "To Have Money and To Be Rich," was dated 1866. Vissering revealed about two others of his pieces of writing that they were written on a popular level similar to that of Harriet Martineau's *Illustrations of Political Economy*.[4] Furthermore, Vissering published an article on "Popular Economics" in 1851, in which he discussed a number of translations of predominantly popular, foreign economics works.[5] In his textbook *Handboek Van Praktische Staathuishoudkunde*, which was used as a text for the teaching of economics at law faculties, Vissering also had addressed himself to an audience wider and more diversified than one consisting solely of university law students.

Sloet Tot Oldhuis provided a Dutch translation of *Économie politique ou Principes de la science des richesse* by Joseph Droz, and described this book as highly suited for the popularization of economics among the Dutch people. He stressed the importance of popular knowledge of economics primarily because general elections had enabled the Dutch population to participate in the government of the country. Sloet Tot Oldhuis provided a Dutch translation of one of Harriet Martineau's fables in his *Tijdschrift Voor Staathuishoudkunde en Statistiek* (vol, III [1846]); he also gave a great deal of publicity to the writings of Mrs. Marcet in the same journal. Sloet Tot Oldhuis also favored the introduction

---

[4] Simon Vissering, "Eene Wereld In 'T Klein," *Herinneringen*, I, 70–89, and "Hoe Kan Men Een Volk Rijk Maken?," *op. cit.*, pp. 89–123; also III, "Geld Hebben En Rijk Zijn," pp. 1–28, and "Het Geld En De Maatschappelijke Ruilingen," pp. 28–44.

[5] Simon Vissering, "Populaire Staathuishoudkunde," *De Gids*, XV (1851), Part I, 1–25.

of economics into the teaching program of elementary schools.[6] For this reason in particular he welcomed the Dutch translation of Richard Whately's *Introductory Lectures on Political Economy*, in 1852. Sloet Tot Oldhuis claimed that Whately had been responsible for the introduction of economics into several thousand public schools in Britain.[7] He also announced and recommended the Dutch translation of another economics book written for use in elementary education programs, namely *Outlines of Social Economy* by William Ellis. His general belief was that education of the lower classes would promote economic progress and sound government, as well as serve to counteract socialistic and communistic tendencies.

Even the interests of Dutch economists in foreign economic literature appear to have been channeled in some measure by their concern with popularization; for Dutch translators of foreign economic writings concentrated their efforts on works devoted to the vulgarization of economic ideas. This may be noted in the list of Dutch translations of economics books presented as Appendix A. A good proportion of the translated works were of a popular nature, for example: three works by Mrs. Marcet, and various works by Harriet Martineau, Richard Whately, Joseph Droz, William Ellis, Frederic Bastiat, and Ferdinand De Hamal among others. This emphasis on the translation of popular works becomes particularly striking when one recalls that the works of Adam Smith, David Ricardo, and Thomas Malthus, as well as major works of McCulloch and of other leading classical economists were never published in the Dutch language.

THE EFFECT OF THE CLEAVAGE BETWEEN ECONOMICS AND LAW UPON CONCEPTIONS OF THE ROLE OF THEORY

On the basis of all that has been said one would surmise that the cleavage between law and economics in Holland, which occurred during the first quarter of the twentieth century, opened

---

[6] See *Tijdschrift Voor Staathuishoudkunde en Statistiek*, IX (1853), 258–269.

[7] See *Tijdschrift Voor Staathuishoudkunde en Statistiek*, VII (1852), 473. It has been stated elsewhere that Bishop Whately instituted the teaching of Economics in more than 4000 schools. See *Jahrbucher fuer Nationaloekonomie und Statistik*, IV (1865), 83.

new possibilities of growth for the economic discipline. The assumption has been made that the educational background as well as the career pursued by an individual influences his attitudes and objectives in regard to his discipline. Seen from this viewpoint neither the training of Dutch economists in law faculties nor the academic appointments of Dutch economists in law faculties was suited to stimulate the supply of theoretical contributions or of contributions of fundamental significance to economic science. The constraints ensuing from the close, academic association of economics and law, two fields whose methods, objectives, and ways of reasoning did not basically lend themselves to integration, served to orient Dutch economists to endeavors other than promoting the discovery of economic knowledge. The information presented in this study indicates that the academic framework of economics, before the cleavage of economics and law, was not conducive to autonomy of economic thinking or to the advancement of economics as a science.

It should be noted, however, that after the 1870's changes took place in the nature of Dutch economics despite the fact that the position of economics in the academic sphere was not modified. The influence of the Austrian School on economic thought in Holland, together with the impact of Pierson on Dutch economics, were outstanding among the factors responsible for modifying the nature and emphasis of Dutch economics during the last quarter of the nineteenth century. Dutch economics professors began to lecture in their courses on the writings of Austrian economists, which apparently channeled the interests of Dutch students, in some measure, into theoretical economics. Dissertations written by Dutch students of economics in the late 1880's and 1890's on such subjects as wages, interest, progressive taxation, and on the theories of Ricardo and Marx, exemplify this tendency.[8] Theoretical analyses, as were presented in the above dissertations, were extremely rare in the period before 1870. The volume and content of articles published in *De Economist* in the late 1880's similarly indicate a shift in interest and emphasis.

[8] C. A. Verrijn Stuart, "Niederlande," in *Die Wirtschaftstheorie Der Gegenwart*, I (Wien, 1927), 147–149. Verrijn Stuart here refers to the dissertations of Ph. Falkenburg on wages (1890), A. P. N. Koolen on interest (1894), A. J. Cohen Stuart on progressive taxation (1889), H. H. Tasman also on taxation (1890), and his own dissertation on the theories of Ricardo and Marx (1890).

Furthermore, Pierson's interests in economics, although he was a self-taught economist, were closely allied to those of W. C. Mees. In regard to theoretical analysis, diversity of interests, scope, objectives, and productivity, the work of Pierson surpassed that of any previous Dutch nineteenth-century economist, even that of W. C. Mees. The nature of Pierson's impact on Dutch economics was both immediate through his writings, and indirect through his students. For example, C. A. Verrijn Stuart, one of Pierson's most faithful disciples, was appointed to a chair for economics at the Technical School of Delft in 1906; it will be recalled that this was the first academic chair for economics in Holland which was not located in a law faculty. One might pose the question of how different the development of Dutch economics would have been, had a man like Pierson, appeared on the Dutch scene about thirty years earlier. Could the backwardness in Dutch economic thinking have been overcome sooner despite the deterrents inherent in the educational system? The information at hand does not provide an answer. Not until the last decades of the nineteenth century did the combined impact of N. G. Pierson and Austrian economics add new dimensions to Dutch economic thought. Thus the interests of Dutch economists gradually became broader as well as more penetrating, which it seems in retrospect, ought to have made the cleavage between economics and law even more compelling.

LIST OF TRANSLATIONS OF FOREIGN ECONOMICS BOOKS INTO DUTCH

The list includes all translations made during the nineteenth century which the writer came across. It is impossible to assert how complete this list may be as there is no systematic way in which one can search for these translations. Titles of books in the original language were usually not cited by the translators, but wherever possible such titles have been supplied. In most instances it is also unknown what edition of the foreign book was used for translation.

TRANSLATIONS OF ENGLISH WRITINGS

1. Tull, Jethro. *The horse-hoeing husbandry* (1733), translated by C. Van Engelen, *De nieuwe wijze van Landbouwen*. 4 vols. Amsterdam, 1762–1765.

2. Smith, Adam. *The Wealth of Nations* (1776), translated by Mr. Dirk Hoola Van Nooten, *Naspeuringen Over De Natuur En Oorzaken Van Den Rijkdom Der Volkeren*. Amsteldam, 1796 (Part I of Book I only).

3. Crauford, George. *The doctrine of equivalents or an explanation of the nature, the value, and the power of money*. Rotterdam, 1794. Translated by Mr. C. Van Breugel, *De leer van het gelijkwaardige of verklaring van den aart, de waarde, en het vermogen van het geld*. 's Hage, 1803.

4. Brougham and Vaux, Henry Peter Brougham. *An Inquiry into the colonial policy of the European Powers*, translated by P. Van IJzendoorn, 1805. (could not find the Dutch title.) Edinburgh, 1803.

5. Marcet, Mrs. Jane. *Conversations on political economy*. 4th edition. London, 1821. Translated from the 4th edition with preface and comments by Mr. H. W. Tydeman, *Grondbeginselen der Staats-Huishoudkunde in Gemeenzame Gesprekken*. Dordrecht, 1825.

6. Senior, Nassau William. *Principes fondamentaux de l'Économie Politique*, edited by Count Arrivabene. Translated from the French with preface and comments by Mr. H. W. Tydeman, *Grondbeginselen der Staathuishoudkunde*. Leiden, 1839.

7. Marcet, Mrs. Jane. *John Hopkins's notions on political economy*. Boston, 1833. Translated from a French edition by Mad. de Cherbuliez, with preface and comments by Mr. H. W. Tydeman, *Jan Hopkins; Gewigtige Waarheden In Den Vorm Van Vertelselen*. Utrecht, 1840.

8. Marcet, Mrs. Jane. (Could not find English title; perhaps it is part

of one of the previous books), *Rijk and Arm*. Deventer (no date or translator given).

9. Peel, Sir Robert. Speech held in the Lower House of Parliament on English Tariff Reforms, January 27, 1846. Translated by Mr. S. Vissering, *Hervorming In Het Engelsche Tarief Van Inkomende Regten*. Amsterdam, 1846.

10. Bentham, Jeremy. *Théorie des peines et des récompenses*, edited by Étienne Dumont. Translated by Mr. B. W. A. E. Sloet Tot Oldhuis from the French, *Handboekje der Staathuishoudkunde*. Deventer, 1851.

11. Ellis, William. *Outlines of social economy*. London, 1846. Translated by H. Hooft Graafland, *Grondtrekken der Staathuishoudkunde*, Utrecht, 1852.

12. Ellis, William. *A few questions on secular education, what it is, and what it ought to be: with an attempt to answer them*. London, 1848. Translated by J. P. Bredius, *De Opvoeding beschouwd als Middel Tot Wering En Vermindering Van Armoede*. Zwolle, 1852.

13. Whately, Richard. *Introductory lectures on political economy*. Translated from the revised edition by W. Sloet Tot Westerholt, *Lessen Tot Inleiding Der Staathuishoudkunde*. Deventer, 1852.

14. Alison, A. and P. W. (English title not available.) Translated with preface by H. W. Tydeman, *De Staatszorg voor de Armen verdedigd en aangeprezen*. Leiden, 1853.

15. McCulloch, J. R. *Essay on the Circumstances which Determine the Rate of Wages*, 1826. Translated with comments by W. Sloet Tot Westerholt, *Over de Omstandigheden Die Den Prijs Der Werkloonen En Den Toestand Der Arbeidende Klassen Bepalen*. Zwolle, 1853.

16. Dunckley, Henry. (English title not available.) Translated by Mr. P. P. Bosse, *De Vrije handelsstaatkunde en haar invloed op Nijverheid en Volkswelvaart*. Hoogezand, 1856.

17. Mill, John Stuart. *On Liberty*. Translator unknown, *Gedachten Over Vrijheid*. Groningen, 1859.

18. Mill, John Stuart. *Principles of Political Economy*, 1848. Translated by Mr. Jacques Oppenheim, *Staathuishoudkunde*. Groningen, 1875–1876.

19. George, Henry. *Progress and Poverty*. Translated by J. W. Straatman, *Vooruitgang en Armoede*. Haarlem, 1882.

20. Jevons, William Stanley. *Political Economy*. Translated by Mr. H. J. Van Leeuwen, *Beginselen der Staathuishoudkunde*. Heusden, 1895.

21. Ely, Richard Theodore. *An Introduction to Political Economy*, 1889. Translated by Mr. D. A. Giel under supervision of Prof. M. W. F. Treub, *Inleiding Tot De Staathuishoudkunde*. Amsterdam, 1897.

TRANSLATIONS OF FRENCH WRITINGS

1. Savary, Jacques. *Le parfait negociant*. Translated by G. Van Broekhuizen, *De Volmaakte Koopman*. Amsterdam, 1683.

2. Condillac, Étienne Bonnot de. *Le Commerce et Le Gouvernement*. Amsterdam, 1776. Translated by Mr. Dirk Hoola Van Nooten, *Koophandel en Staatsbestuur*. Utrecht, 1782.

3. Droz, Joseph. *Applications de la morale a la politique*. Paris, 1825. Translated by Pieter de Haan, *De Grondslagen Der Maatschappij*. Leiden, 1826.

4. Bastiat, Frédéric. *Sophismes économiques.* Translated from the second French edition by W. M. Boer, *Staathuishoudkundige Drogredenen.* Utrecht, 1847.

5. Say, Jean Baptiste. *Catéchisme D'Économie Politique.* Translated by Mr. H. Houck, *Beginselen der Volkshuishoudkunde.* Deventer, 1847.

6. Bastiat, Frédéric. (French title not available.) Translated by Mr. W. R. Boer, *Kapitaal en Interest.* Utrecht, 1849.

7. Bastiat, Frédéric. (French title not available.) Translated by Mr. W. R. Boer, *Dat Verwenschte Geld.* Utrecht, 1849.

8. Bastiat, Frédéric. *Ce qu'on voit et ce qu'on ne voit pas.* No translator known, *Wat Men Ziet En Wat Men Niet Ziet.* Dordrecht, 1850.

9. Blanqui, Adolph Jérôme. *Précis élémentaire d'économie politique.* No translator known, *Beknopt Overzigt Van De Eerste Beginselen Der Staathuishoudkunde.* Deventer, 1850.

10. Droz, Joseph. *Économie politique, ou Principes de la science des richesse.* Paris, 1829. Translated with preface by Mr. B. W. A. E. Sloet Tot Oldhuis, *Staathuishoudkunde of Beginselen Van De Leer Des Rijkdoms.* Deventer, 1849, a second edition in 1850.

11. De Hamal, Ferdinand. (French title not available.) No translator known, *Beginselen Der Staathuishoudkunde, Ten Gebruike Van Jonge Lieden, Die Zich Aan Eene Staatkundige of Administratieve Loopbaan Willen Toewijden.* Deventer, 1850.

12. Bastiat, Frédéric. (No French title available.) Translated by Mr. C. M. A. Van Der Aa, *De Staat, Het Beschermend Stelsel, En Het Communisme.* Leeuwarden, 1851.

13. Bastiat, Frédéric. (French title not available.) No translator known, *Eigendom en Berooving.* Franeker, 1851.

14. Chevalier, Michel. (French title not available.) Translated by D. P. H. Aberson, *Het Beschermend Stelsel.* Tiel, 1851.

15. Bastiat, Frédéric. *Gratuité du crédit.* Paris, 1850. Translated by Mr. G. M. A. Simon Van Der Aa (a discussion between Bastiat and Proudhon), *Krediet Om Niet.* Leeuwarden, 1852.

16. Bastiat, Frédéric. (French title not available.) No translator known, *Roof en Wet.* Franeker, 1852.

17. Bastiat, Frédéric. (French title not available.) Translated by Mr. C. M. A. Simon Van Der Aa, *Onvereenigbaarheid van Betrekkingen gevolgd door twee voorlezingen over de Beteugling der Vereeniging van Nijverheid en over de Belasting op de Dranken.* Leeuwarden, 1852.

18. Bastiat, Frédéric. (French title not available.) Translated by Mr. C. M. A. Simon Van Der Aa, *De Doctorale Graad en het Socialismus.* Leeuwarden, 1852.

19. Bienqui, Adolphe Jérôme. *Histoire de l'économie politique en Europe,* 1837. Translated after the third edition by Mr. J. Versfelt, *Geschiedenis Der Staathuishoudkunde Van De Vroegste Tijd Tot Op Onze Dagen.* 1852.

20. Bastiat, Frédéric. *Harmonies économiques.* Paris, 1850. Translated by Mr. C. M. A. Simon Van Der Aa after the second edition, *Staathuishoudkundige Harmonien.* Sneek, 1853.

21. Say, Jean Baptiste. *Traité d'économie politique.* Paris, 1803. No translator known, *Ontwikkeling van Beginselen der Staathuishoudkunde,* eenv. verklaring van de wijze waarop de rijkdom voortgebracht, verdeeld en verbruikt wordt. Deventer, 1857.

22. Baudrillart, Henri Joseph Léon. *Manuel d'économie politique.*

Translated by W. A. Viruly Verbrugge, *Handboek der Staathuishoudkunde.*
Haarlem, 1859.

23. Garnier, Joseph. *Premières notions d'économie politique.* No translator known, *Beknopte Verhandeling over de Beginselen Der Staathuishoudkunde.* Rotterdam, 1859.

24. Rondelet, A. (French title not available.) Translated by Mr. G. T. N. Gori, *Grondtrekken Der Staathuishoudkunde.* Amsterdam, 1869.

25. Block, Maurice. *Petit manuel d'économie pratique.* Translated by W. A. Coolen, *Praatjes Over Volkshuishouding,* 's Hertogenbosch, 1873.

26. Block, Maurice. *Doctrines économiques.* No translator known, *Grondbeginselen Der Volkshuishoudkunde.* Second edition, 's Hertogenbosch, no date.

27. Martineau, Harriet. *Illustrations of Political Economy.* Translated into Dutch in 1877, translator and Dutch title not available.

28. Noël, Octave Eugène. (French title not available.) Translator not known, *Maatschappij en het Huisgezin,* Losse Bladen uit het Groote Boek Der Staathuishoudkunde. Tiel, 1880.

29. Lavelaye, Emile. *Eléments d'économie politique.* Paris, 1882. Translated by Mr. J. D. Veegens, *Beginselen Van Staathuishoudkunde.* Haarlem, 1884.

TRANSLATIONS OF GERMAN WRITINGS

1. Sueszmilch, J. P. *Die Goettliche Ordnung in den Veraenderungen des menschlichen Geschlechts aus der Geburt, Tod, und Fortpflanzung desselben erwiesen,* 1742. No translator known, *De goddelijke orde, heerschende in de veranderingen van het menschelijke geslacht, uit de geboorte, het sterven, en de voortplanting van hetzelve beweezen.* Translated in 4 volumes after the second edition of 1761–1762. Amsteldam, 1770–1772.

2. Von Justi, Johann Heinrich Gottlob. *Vollstaendige abhandlung von den manufacturen und fabriken.* No translator known, *Verhandelingen over de Manufacturen en Fabrijken.* Utrecht, 1782.

3. Von Schloezer, August Ludwig. *Theorie der statistiek, Nebst Ideen ueber des studium der politik ueberhaupt.* Goettingen, 1804. Translated by Mr. H. M. Tydeman, *Theorie Der Statistiek of Staats-kunde,* second edition. Groningen, 1814.

4. Nebenius, C. F. (German title not available.) No translator known, *Denkbeelden Nopens De Bevordering Van Nijverheid Door Onderwijs.* 's Gravenhage, 1842.

5. Schulze, F. O. (German title not available.) Translated by E. C. Enkelaar, *Volkshuishoudkunde Voor Allen Die In Landbouw en Nijverheid Belang Stellen.* Zwolle, 1858.

6. Kalle, F. (German title not available.) No translator known, *Aanleiding Tot Huiselijke En Maatschappelijke Welvaart Met Het Oog Op De Socialistische Beweging Dezer Dagen,* Deventer, 1878.

TRANSLATIONS OF ITALIAN WRITINGS

1. Verri, Pietro. *Meditazioni sulla Economia Politica.* Translated by Mr. Dirk Hoola Van Nooten, from the French, *De Staatkundige Oeconomie.* Leiden, 1801.

SELECTED BIBLIOGRAPHY

PRIMARY SOURCES

Books and Pamphlets

Ackersdijck, Jan. *Bedenkingen over de Korenwetten.* Utrecht, 1835.
— *Nederlands Financien.* – Nationale Schuld. Amsterdam, 1843.
— *Nederlands Muntwezen.* Utrecht, 1845.
— *Over Belastingen en Bezuiniging.* Utrecht, 1849.
Asser, T. M. C. *Verhandeling Over Het Staathuishoudkundig Begrip der Waarde.* Amsterdam, ˙˙˙8.
Baert, J. F. B. *Adam Smith En Zijn Onderzoek Naar Den Rijkdom Der Volkeren.* Leiden, 1858.
D'Aulnis De Bourouill, J. *Het Inkomen Der Maatschappij.* Leiden, 1874.
— *Het Katheder-Socialisme.* Utrecht, 1878.
De Bosch Kemper, J. *Geschiedkundig Onderzoek Naar De Armoede in Ons Vaderland.* Haarlem, 1851.
— *De Uitbreiding Van Het Hooger Onderwijs te Amsterdam.* Amsterdam, 1873.
De Bruyn Kops, J. L. *Beginselen Van Staathuishoudkunde.* Amsterdam, 1850.
— *Beginselen Van Staathuishoudkunde.* 2 vols. Fifth edition. 's Gravenhage, 1873.
— *Korte Beschouwingen Over Het Armwezen.* Leyden en Amsterdam, 1851.
— *Over het Beginsel van Armenverzorging door den Staat.* Leiden– Amsterdam, 1852.
Elink Sterk, A., Jr. *Eenige Bedenkingen op het Geschrift van Mr. J. L. De Bruyn Kops over het Beginsel van Armenverzorging door den Staat.* 's Gravenhage, 1852.
Greven, Hendrik Baren. *De Ontwikkeling Der Bevolkingsleer.* Leiden, 1875.
Hamaker, Hendrik Jacob. *De Historische School in de Staathuishoudkunde.* Leiden, 1870.
Heymans, G. *Karakter en Methode der Staathuishoudkunde.* Leiden, 1880.
Van Hogendorp, Gijsbert Karel. *Gedagten Over 'S Lands Finantien.* Amsterdam, 1802.
— *Bijdragen Tot De Huishouding Van Staat.* 10 vols. 's Gravenhage, 1817–1825.
— *Bijdragen Tot De Huishouding Van Staat.* Tweede Verbeterde Uitgave Onder Toezicht Van Mr. J. R. Thorbecke. Zalt-Bommel, 1854–1855.

— *Brieven en Gedenkschriften*. Edited by Mr. H. Graaf Van Hogendorp. Vol. IV. 's Gravenhage, 1887.

Hooft Graafland, H. *De Staatsschulden Getoetst Aan De Beginselen der Staathuishoudkunde*. Utrecht, 1851.

Van Houten, S. *Verhandeling Over De Waarde*. Groningen, 1859.

Luttenberg, G. *Proeve Van Onderzoek omtrent het Armwezen in ons Vaderland*, Amsterdam, 1841.

Luzac, Elias. *Hollands Rijkdom*. 4 vols. Leyden, 1780–1783.

Mees, W. C. *Proeve Eener Geschiedenis Van Het Bankwexen In Nederland Gedurende Den Tijd Der Republiek*. Rotterdam, 1838.

— *De Werkinrigtingen Voor Armen Uit Een Staathuishoudkundig Oogpunt Beschouwd*. Rotterdam, 1844.

— *Overzicht Van Eenige Hoofdstukken Der Staathuishoudkunde*. Amsterdam, 1866.

Pierson, N. G. *De Toekomst Der Nederlandsche Bank*. Haarlem, 1863.

— *Leerboek Der Staathuishoudkunde*. 2 vols. Haarlem, 1896. Second edition.

— *Verspreide Economische Geschriften*. 6 vols. Haarlem, 1910–1911.

Portielje, D. A. *De Handel Van Nederland in 1844*. Amsterdam, 1844.

— and S. Vissering. *Geschiedenis Der Tariefhervorming in Engeland*. Amsterdam, 1847.

Van Rees, Otto. *Verhandeling Over De Aanwijsing der Politieke Gronden en Maximen van de Republiek van Holland en West-Vriesland door Pieter de la Court*. Utrecht, 1851.

— *Verhandeling Over De Verdiensten Van Gijsbert Karel Van Hogendorp*. Utrecht, 1854.

— *Geschiedenis der Nederlandsche Volksplantingen in Noord-Amerika, Beschouwd Uit Het Oogpunt Der Koloniale Politiek*. Tiel, 1855.

— *Redevoering Over De Staathuishoudkundige Geschiedenis Van Nederland*. Zutphen, 1858.

— *Redevoering Over De Wetenschap Der Statistiek*. Utrecht, 1860.

— *Geschiedenis Der Staathuishoudkunde in Nederland*. 2 vols. Utrecht, 1865–1868.

Smith, Adam. *An Inquiry into the Nature and Causes of the Wealth of Nations*. Edited by Edwin Cannan, The Modern Library. New York, 1937.

Van Stolk, Thomas. *De Stelsels der Staathuishoudkundigen Omtrent Grondrente Ontvouwd en Beoordeeld*. Rotterdam, 1858.

Tydeman, H. W. *Verhandeling over de Vraag: Waren de Inrigtingen der Gilden....* Middelburg, 1821.

—, J. Heemskerk and J. W. Tydeman. *Denkbeelden Omtrent Eene Wettelijke Regeling Van Het Armwezen in Nederland*. Amsterdam, 1850.

Vissering, Simon. *Handboek Van Praktische Staathuishoudkunde*. 2 vols. Amsterdam, 1860–1865.

— *Handboek Van Praktische Staathuishoudkunde*. 2 vols. Fourth edition. Amsterdam, 1878.

— *Herinneringen*. 3 vols. Amsterdam, 1863–1872.

— *Verzamelde Geschriften*. 2 vols. Leiden, 1889.

— "Hoe Kan Men Een Volk Rijk Maken?," *Herinneringen*, I, 89–123.

— "Eene Wereld In 'T Klein," *Herinneringen*, I, 70–89.

— "De Vrije Graanhandel," *Herinneringen*, II, 1–64.

— "Over Vrijheid, Het Grondbeginsel Der Staathuishoudkunde," *Verzamelde Geschriften*, II (Leiden, 1889), 142–171.

156   SELECTED BIBLIOGRAPHY

— "Over Werkloonen en Volksvoeding," *Herinneringen*, II, 268–292.
— "Regeling Van Het Armwezen," *Herinneringen*, II, 186–268.
— "De Nederlandsche Bank Gedurende Haar Vijftigjarig Bestaan,"
Herinneringen, III, 44–131.
— "Geld Hebben En Rijk Zijn," *Herinneringen*, III, 1–28.
— "Het Geld En De Maatschappelijke Ruilingen," *Herinneringen*, III,
28–44.
Van Voorthuysen, E. *De Directe Belastingen*. Utrecht, 1848.

Articles

Ackersdijck, Jan. "Redevoering over Adam Smith," *Tijdschrift Voor
Staathuishoudkunde en Statistiek*, II (1843), 1–18.
De Bruyn Kops, J. L. "Het Onderwijs In De Staathuishoudkunde," *De
Economist*, VI (1857), 129–142.
— "Eenige Gedachten Over De Economische Wetenschap," *De Econo-
mist*, XI (1862), 1–17.
— "Toespraak by de opening der lessen in de Staathuishoudkunde aan
de Polytechnische School, 1864," *De Economist*, XIV (1865), 1–21.
— "De Verdeeling Van Den Maatschappelijken Rijkdom," *De Econo-
mist*, Het Bijblad (1867), pp. 382–408.
— "Toespraak Bij De Opening Van Den Cursus In De Staathuishoud-
kunde 1867–68," *De Economist*, XVII (1868), Part I, 1–32, 150–159.
— "Aan Den Lezer," *De Economist*, XXV (1876), Part I.
— "Michel Chevalier," *De Economist*, XXIX (1880), Part I, 65–75.
Buys, J. T. "Over Arbeidsloonen," *De Economist*, II (1853), 371–384.
Mees, W. C. "Eenige Opmerkingen over de Gevolgen der Vermeerderde
Voortbrenging van Goud," *Staatkundig en Staathuishoudkundig Jaar-
boekje*, VII (1855), 302–310.
— "Hebben wij wel Gedaan, met het Zilver tot eenigen Muntstandaard
aan te Nemen?," *Tijdschrift Voor Staathuishoudkunde en Statistiek*,
XIV (1857), 249–274.
— "Maatregelen Der Regering Tegen Den Omloop Van Vreemde Munt,"
De Economist, IX (1860), 373–388.
— "De Muntstandaard in Verband met de Pogingen tot Invoering van
Eenheid van Munt," *Verslagen en Mededeelingen der Koninklijke Aka-
demie van Wetenschappen*, Adfeeling Letterkunde, XII (1869), Amster-
dam, 1–45.
— "Opmerkingen Omtrent Gelijke Verdeeling Van Belasting," *Ver-
slagen en Mededeelingen der Koninklijke Akademie van Wetenschappen*,
Afdeeling Letterkunde, V (1874), Amsterdam.
— "Poging Tot Verduidelijking Van Eenige Begrippen In De Staat-
huishoudkunde," *Verslagen en Mededeelingen der Koninklijke Akademie van Wetenschappen*, Afdeeling Letterkunde, VII (1877), Amsterdam.
— "Eene Briefwisseling Tusschen Gijsbert Karel Van Hogendorp en
Prof. Jan Ackersdijck," *Economisch-Historisch Jaarboek*, XII (1926),
100–124.
Pierson, N. G. "Vrijheid of Beperking," *Verspreide Economische Geschriften*, IV, 403–441.
— "De Inkomstenbelasting," *Verspreide Economische Geschriften*, V,
20–57.

Van Rees, Otto. "Antwoord Over De Bank-Kwestie Aan Den Heer Mr. S. Vissering," *De Economist*, XII (1863), 448–452.
— "De Regeering En De Nijverheid," *Staatkundig en Staathuishoudkundig Jaarboekje*, VIII (1856), 361–372; XII (1860), 260–278; XVII (1865), 341–360.
Sloet Tot Oldhuis, B. W. A. E. "De Belasting op de Inkomsten," *Jaarboek Voor Staathuishoudkunde en Statistiek*, XXVIII (1875), 176–185.
Vissering, Simon. "Open Brief Over De Bank-Kwestie Aan Den Heer Mr. O. Van Rees," *De Economist*, XII (1863), 373–387.

Periodicals

Bijdragen Tot De Staathuishoudkunde en Statistiek, 1836–1838. Edited by G. M. Wttenwaall.
De Economist, 1852–. Edited by J. L. De Bruyn Kops until 1887.
De Gids, 1837–. (Examined volumes from 1837–1876).
De Koopman of bijdragen ten opbouw van Nederlands koophandel en zeevaart, 1768–1776.
Magazijn Voor Het Armwezen, 1817–1822. Edited by H. W. Tydeman.
Overzicht der Werkzaamheden van de Afdeeling Koophandel der Maatschappij Felix Meritis, 1850–1855.
Staatkundig en Staathuishoudkundig Jaarboekje, 1849–1884. Edited by J. De Bosch Kemper.
Tijdschrift Voor Staathuishoudkunde en Statistiek, 1841–1875. Edited by B. W. A. E. Sloet Tot Oldhuis.

SECONDARY SOURCES

Books and Pamphlets

Algemeene Bibliotheek vervattende Naauwkeurige Berigten Van De Voornaamste Werken In De Geleerde Wereld Alom Van Tijd tot Tijd Uitkomende. Vol. I. Amsterdam, 1777.
Baasch, Ernst. *Hollaendische Wirtschaftsgeschichte*. Jena, 1927.
Barbour, Violet. *Capitalism in Amsterdam in the Seventeenth Century*. The Johns Hopkins University Studies in Historical and Political Science, LXVII (Baltimore, 1950), 1–173.
Blok, P. J. *Geschiedenis Van Het Nederlandsche Volk*. 4 vols. Derde, Herziene Druk, Leiden, 1923–1926.
Boer, M. W. R. *Frederic Bastiat, Eene Staathuishoudkundige Studie*. Utrecht, 1860.
Bordewijk, H. W. C. *Theoretisch-Historische Inleiding Tot De Economie*. Den Haag, 1931.
Van der Borght, Richard. "A History of Banking in the Netherlands," *A History of Banking in all the Leading Nations*, IV (New York, 1896), 260–324.
Brugmans, I. J. *De Arbeidende Klasse in Nederland in de 19e Eeuw*, 's Gravenhage, 1925.
— *Welvaart en Historie*. 's Gravenhage, 1950.
Buddingh, D. *Over Industrie- en Handelakademieen in Verdere Inrigtingen van Onderwijs Ter Bevordering Van Nijverheid en Handel in Europa*. Amsterdam & Delft, 1842.

158   SELECTED BIBLIOGRAPHY

Cossa, Luigi. *An Introduction to the Study of Political Economy.* London 1893.
Diepenhorst, P. A. *De Klassieke School In De Economie.* Amsterdam, 1904.
— *Leerboek Van De Economie.* Vol. I. Zutphen, 1946.
Elster, Ludwig. "Der Bevoelkerungsstand und die Bevoelkerungs-bewegung der neuesten Zeit bis zum Ausbruch des Weltkrieges," *Handwoerterbuch Der Staatswissenschaften,* Vierte Auflage, III (Jena, 1924), 688–689.
Elzinga, S. *Het Economisch Hoger Onderwijs Als Vertegenwoordiger Der Moderne Cultuur.* Wassenaar, 1941.
Evers, J. C. G. *Bijdrage Tot De Bevolkingsleer Van Nederland.* 's Gravenhage, 1882.
Everwijn, J. C. A. *Beschrijving van Handel en Nijverheid in Nederland.* Den Haag, 1912.
Falkenburg, Ph. "Armengesetzgebund in den Niederlanden," *Handwoerterbuch Der Staatswissenschaften,* Dritte Auflage, II (Jena, 1909), 113–119.
Furnivall, J. S. *Netherlands India.* Cambridge and New York, 1944.
Gedenkschrift Ter Herinnering Aan De Opening Der Nederlandsche Handels-Hoogeschool Te Rotterdam. Delft, 1913.
Goslings, A. *Koning Willem I Als Verlicht Despoot.* Baarn, 1902.
Hirschfeld, Hans Max. *Het Ontstaan Van Het Moderne Bankwezen In Nederland.* Rotterdam, 1932.
Huizinga, J. *Geschiedenis Der Universiteit Gedurende De Derde Eeuw Van Haar Bestaan,* 1814–1914, *Academia Groninga,* I (Groningen, 1914). Also, in Huizinga's *Verzamelde Werken,* VIII (Haarlem, 1951), 36–340.
The Jewish Encyclopedia. Vol. VIII. New York and London, 1904.
De Jong, A. M. *Geschiedenis Van De Nederlandsche Bank.* Haarlem, 1930.
— "The Origin and Foundation of the Netherlands Bank," *History of the Principal Public Banks,* collected J. G. Van Dillen. The Hague, 1934, pp. 319–335.
— *Inleiding Tot Het Bevolkingsvraagstuk.* 'S-Gravenhage, 1946.
Kernkamp, G. W. De Utrechtsche Hoogeschool van 1815 tot 1877, *De Utrechtsche Universiteit,* 1815–1936, II (Utrecht, 1936), 73–129.
King, Gregory. *Natural and Political Observations and Conclusions upon the State and Condition of England, 1696,* in *Two Tracts.* Reprinted by The Johns Hopkins Press, Baltimore, 1936.
Van Der Kooy, Tjalling Pieter. *Hollands Stapelmarkt En Haar Verval.* Amsterdam, 1931.
Laspeyres, Etienne. *Geschichte Der Volkswirtschaftlichen An-Schauungen Der Niederlaender.* Leipzig, 1863.
McCulloch, J. R. *A Select Collection of Scarce and Valuable Tracts on Commerce.* London, 1859.
Van Malsen, W. L. *Frederic Bastiat En Zijn Nederlandsche Beoordeelaars.* Rotterdam, 1921.
Van Der Mandele, K. E. *Het Liberalisme in Nederland.* Arnhem, 1933.
Mansvelt, W. M. F. *Geschiedenis Van De Nederlandsche Handel-Maatschappij.* 2 vols. Haarlem, 1924–1926.
Mees, W. C. *Man Van De Daad – Mr Marten Mees en de Opkomst Van Rotterdam.* Rotterdam, 1946.
Molster, J. A. *Geschiedenis der Staathuishoudkunde van de Vroegste Tijden tot Heden.* Amsterdam, 1851.

Nebenius, C. F. *Denkbeelden Nopens De Bevordering Van Nijverheid Door Onderwijs*, uit het Hoogduitsch door D. Buddingh. 'S Gravenhage, 1842.

Van Nierop, Leonie. *De Bevolkingsbeweging Der Nederlandsche Stad.* Amsterdam, 1905.

Nieuw Nederlandsch Biographisch Woordenboek. 10 vols. Edited by C. P. Molhuysen, P. J. Blok, *et al.* Leiden, 1911–1937.

Palyi, Melchoir. "The Introduction of Adam Smith On the Continent, *Adam Smith*, 1776–1926. Chicago,1926.

Peel, Robert. *Redevoering van Sir Robert Peel Over De Tariefshervorming.* Translated by S. Vissering. Amsterdam, 1846.

Polak, N. J. "Het Economisch Hoger Onderwijs," *Verspreide Geschriften*, II (Purmerend, 1933), 489–494.

Polak, Siegfried. *Beknopte Geschiedenis Der Staathuishoudkunde in Theorie en Praktijk.* Groningen, 1919.

Posthumous, N. W. *Documenten Betreffende De Buitenlandsche Handelspolitiek Van Nederland In De Negentiende Eeuw.* Vol. I. 'S-Gravenhage, 1919.

— "De Faculteit Der Handelswetenschappen," *Gedenkboek Van Het Athenaeum En De Universiteit Van Amsterdam 1632–1932.* Amsterdam, 1932.

Pringsheim, Otto. *Beitraege Zur Wirtschaftlichen Entwickelungsgeschichte der Vereinigten Niederlande im 17. und 18. Jahrhundert.* Leipzig, 1890.

Quack, H. P. G. *Uit Den Kring Der Gemeenschap.* Amsterdam, 1899.

— *Herinneringen.* Tweede Druk. Amsterdam, 1915.

Romein, Jan en Annie. *Erflaters Von Onze Beschaving.* Amsterdam, 1939.

De Rooy, E. W. *Geschiedenis der Staathuishoudkunde in Europa.* Amsterdam, 1851.

Russell, H. B. *International Monetary Conferences*, New York, 1898.

Schumpeter, Joseph A. *History of Economic Analysis.* New York, 1954.

Siegenbeek, Matthys. *Geschiedenis der Leidsche Hoogeschool.* Vol. I. Leiden, 1829

Sillem, Jerome Alexander. *De Politieke en Staathuishoudkundige Werkzaamheid van Isaac Alexander Gogel.* Amsterdam, 1864.

Sneller, Z. W. *Economische en Sociale Denkbeelden In Nederland In Den Aanvang Der Negentiende Eeuw*, 1814–1830. Haarlem, 1922.

— *De Ontwikkeling Der Nederlandsche Export-Industrie.* Haarlem, 1925.

— *Rede Uitgesproken Ter Gelegenheid Van De Herdenking* op 8 November, 1938, Van De Stichting Der Nederlandsche Handels-Hoogeschool.

— *Geschiedenis Van De Nederlandsche Landbouw 1795–1940.* Tweede Druk. Groningen–Djakarta, 1951.

Toespraak, H. "Hulde Ter Nagedachtenis Van Mr. O. Van Rees," Gehouden in een Buitengewone Vergadering der Vereeniging ter Bevordering Van Nuttige Kennis. Utrecht, 1868.

Treub, M. W. F. *Een Drietal Hoofdstukken Uit De Geschiedenis Der Staathuishoudkunde.* Haarlem, 1899.

Tydeman, H. W. Introduction to *Grondbeginselen Der Staats-Huishoudkunde.* Dordrecht, 1825. Dutch translation of Mrs. Marcet's *Conversations on Political Economy.*

Valkhoff, J. *Rechtssociologische Elementen In De Nederlandse Rechtswetenschap Van De XIXde Eeuw.* Haarlem, 1955.

Vandenbosch, Amry and Samuel J. Eldersveld. *Governments of the Netherlands*. Lexington, 1947.

Van Der Vegte, H. "De Staathuishoudkunde in het Kader van het Hooger Onderwijs," *Sociaal-Economische Opstellen Aangeboden Aan Mr. H. B. Greven*. Haarlem, 1916, pp. 375–390.

Verberne, L. C. J. *De Nederlandsche Arbeidersbeweging In De Negentiende Eeuw*. Amsterdam, 1940.

Verrijn Stuart, C. A. *Inleiding Tot De Beoefening Der Statistiek*. 4 vols. Haarlem, 1910.

— "The History and Development of Statistics in the Netherlands," *The History of Statistics*, by John Koren. New York, 1918, pp. 427–445.

Verrijn Stuart, G. M. *Geld, Crediet, en Bankwezen*. Vol. II. Fifth edition. Wassenaar, 1943.

Verviers, Emile. *De Nederlandsche Handelspolitiek Tot aan de Toepassing der Vrijhandelsbeginselen*. Leiden, 1914.

Vissering, Simon. "Levensbericht Van Mr. Willem Cornelis Mees," *Verzamelde Geschriften*, I (Leiden, 1889), 221–262.

— "De Nederlandsche Bank Onder Het Bestuur Van Mr. W. C. Mees," *Verzamelde Geschriften*, II, 302–335.

— "Studieen over Hooger Onderwijs," *Herinneringen*, III, 149–398.

— "Mr. O. Van Rees," *Herinneringen*, III, 142–149.

Van Der Vlught, W. "De Geestelijke Wetenschappen," *Historisch Gedenkboek Eene Halve Eeuw*, 1848–1898. Amsterdam, 1898, pp. 43–48.

Weeveringh, J. J. *Handleiding Tot De Geschiedenis Der Staatsschulden*. Vol. I. Haarlem, 1852.

Wetten, besluiten, en beschikkingen betreffende Hoger Onderwijs en Wetenschappen. Edited by P. Van Werkum. Dertiende Druk. Zwolle, 1954.

Wilson, Charles. *Anglo-Dutch Commerce & Finance in the Eighteenth Century*. Cambridge, 1941.

The World of Learning, 1957. Eighth edition. London, 1957.

Wright, H. R. C. *Free Trade and Protection in the Netherlands 1816–1830*. Cambridge, 1955.

Zimmerman, L. J. *Geschiedenis van het Economisch Denken*. Amsterdam, 1947.

Articles

D'Aulnis De Bourouill, J. "Levensbericht van N. G. Pierson," *Jaarboek der Koninklijke Akademie van Wetenschappen*. Amsterdam, 1911.

Buys, J. T. "Levensbericht van Mr. S. Vissering," *Jaarboek Van De Koninklijke Akademie Van Wetenschappen*. Amsterdam, 1889, pp. 26–59

Carter, Alice. "The Dutch and the English Public Debt in 1777," *Economica*, XX (1953), 159–162.

— "Dutch Foreign Investment, 1738–1800," *Economica*, XX (1953), 322–341.

Fruin, J. A. "Levensbericht van Mr. Otto Van Rees," *Levensberichten Der Afgestorvene Medeleden van de Maatschappij der Nederlandsche Letter-Kunde*. Leiden, 1869, pp. 123–160.

Goedhart, C. "Honderd Jaar Openbare Financien," *De Economist*, C (1952), 958–996.

Greven, H. B. "Simon Vissering," *Almanak Van Het Leidsche Studentencorps*, 1889, pp. 359–367.

Hennipman, P. "J. L. De Bruyn Kops," *De Economist*, C (1952), 785–815.

Huizinga, J. "Der Einfluss Deutschlands in der Geschichte der Niederländischen Kultur," *Archiv für Kulturgeschichte*, XVI (Berlin, 1926), 208–222.

De Jong, F. J. "Phoenix Vrijhandel: Van Het Naieve Naar Het Critische Vrijhandelspunt," *De Economist*, C (1952), 924–958.

Koenen, H. J. "Ter Gedachtenis Van Mr. J. Ackersdijck," *Jaarboek Van De Koninklijke Akademie Van Wetenschappen*. Amsterdam, 1861, pp. 121–129.

Kuznets, Simon. "Quantitative Aspects of the Economic Growth of, Nations," *Economic Development and Cultural Change*, V, No. 1 (October, 1956).

Lambers, H. W. "Honderd Jaar Goede Bedoelingen (De Economist 1852–1952)," *De Economist*, C (1952), 815–828.

Limperg, Th. Jr. "De Faculteit Der Economische Wetenschappen Der Universiteit Van Amsterdam," *Jaarboek der Universiteit*, 1946–47. Amsterdam, pp. 1–16.

Mees, W. C. "Levensberight van Mr. Jan Ackersdijck," *Levensberigten Der Afgestorvene Medeleden Van De Maatschappij Der Nederlandsche Letterkunde*. Leiden, 1862, pp. 25–47.

Pierson, N. G. "Levensbericht van Mr. W. C. Mees," *Verspreide Economische Geschriften*, II (Haarlem, 1910), 326–359.

— "Economisch Overzicht," *Verspreide Economische Geschriften*, II, 487–516.

Quarles Van Ufford, K. J. W. "Levensbericht van Mr. Jacob Leonard De Bruyn Kops," *Levensberichten Der Afgestorvene Medeleden Van De Maatschappij der Nederlandsche Letterkunde*. Leiden, 1889, pp. 29–56.

— "In Memoriam, Mr. J. L. De Bruyn Kops," *De Economist*, XXXVI (1887), Part II, 862–867.

Van Rees, Otto. "De Wetenschappelijke Werkzaamheid van Mr. J· Ackersdijck," *Utrechtsche Studenten-Almanak*, 1862. Utrecht, pp. 169–212.

— "Het Collegie van Adriaan Kluit Over de Statistiek Van Nederland," *Tijdschrift Voor Staathuishoudkunde en Statistiek*, XII (1855), 245–263.

Sickenga, F. N. "Staathuishoudkunde in het begin der negentiende eeuw hier te lande," *Tijdschrift Voor Staathuishoudkunde en Statistiek*, XXVI (1866), 165–173.

Sloet Tot Oldhuis, B. W. A. E. "De Vier Faculteiten," *Tijdschrift Voor Staathuishoudkunde en Statistiek*, XVIII (1859), 407–427.

— "Mr. J. Ackersdijck," *Tijdschrift Voor Staathuishoudkunde en Statistiek*, XXI (1861), 169–185.

Tydeman, J. W. "Levensberigt van Mr. Hendrik Willem Tydeman," *Levensberigten van de Afgestorvene Leden der Maatschappij der Nederlandsche Letterkunde*. Leiden, 1863, pp. 403–450.

Verrijn Stuart, C. A. "Niederlande," *Die Wirtschaftstheorie Der Gegenwart*, I (Wien, 1927), 142–151.

Verrijn Stuart, G. M. "Die Industriepolitik der Niederlaendischen Regierung," *Kieler Vortraege* gehalten im Institut fuer Weltwirtschaft an der Universitaet Kiel, 1936.

— "Nieuwe Regeling Van Het Nederlandsche Muntwezen," *De Economist*, XCV (1947), 309–360.

— "Honderd Jaar Geld – En Bankwezen," *De Economist*, C (1952), 880–912.

"Simon Vissering," *Eigen Haard*, No. 41 (Haarlem, 1879), pp. 411–414.

Vissering, Simon. "Levensbericht Van O. Van Rees," *Jaarboek van de Koninklijke Akademie van Wetenschappen*. Amsterdam, 1868, pp. 57–74.

— "De Statistiek Aan De Hoogeschool," *De Gids*, No. II (1877), pp. 1–15.

— "Frederic Bastiat," *De Gids*, XV, Part II (1851), 269–303.

— "Populaire Staathuishoudkunde," *De Gids*, XV, Part I (1851), 1–25.

De Vries, F. "Honderd Jaar Theoretische Economie," *De Economist*, C (1952), 828–880.

Te Water, J. W. "A. Kluit – Levensbericht," *Handelingen Der Jaarlijksche Vergadering Van De Maatschappij Der Nederlandsche Letterkunde*. Leyden, 1807, pp. 2–8.

Wilson, Charles. "The Economic Decline of the Netherlands," *The Economic History Review*, IX, No. 2 (May, 1939), 111–128.